HOLDING ON TO HEAVEN

While Your Friend Goes Through Hell

HOLDING ON TO HEAVEN

While Your Friend Goes Through Hell

BY CONNIE NEAL

WORD PUBLISHING

NASHVILLE

A Thomas Nelson Company

PUBLISHED BY WORD PUBLISHING
Nashville, TN

Unless otherwise indicated, Scripture quotations used in this book are from the Holy Bible, New International Version (NIV). Copyright © 1973, 1978, 1984, International Bible Society. Used by permission of Zondervan Bible Publishers. All rights reserved.

Scripture quotations noted NASB are from the New American Standard Bible. Copyright © 1960, 1962, 1963, 1968, 1971, 1973, 1975, 1977, The Lockman Foundation. Used by permission.

Published in association with Sealy M. Yates, Literary Agent, Orange, California
Printed in the United States of America

99 00 01 02 03 04 05 06 QBP 9 8 7 6 5 4 3 2 1

CONTENTS

Holding on to Heaven
While Your Friend Goes Through Hell

CHAPTER ONE

What Difference Can You Make?
Considering Your Potential Moral Obligations as a Friend

*I*n the fall of 1976 Warren Shank hoped to change the world. As a grad student fresh out of Westmont College and studying to get his teaching credentials, Warren set out to start a Young Life club. He believed that befriending one young person and making a positive impact in that life could make a lifelong difference. So he set out to find a young man who needed a friend.

Warren volunteered to coach the cross-country team on his former high school campus. He wasn't much of a runner, so he prayed, "Lord, please have the slowest guy on the cross-country team be the guy you want me to make friends with." Warren was right about his lack of ability to keep up with the leaders of the pack. He found himself trudging along with the guys at the tail end. He fell into pace with one guy who was wearing a pair of shoes definitely not made for running. Mark Knoble was quiet, didn't open up quickly, and showed no interest in attending a Young Life club. But Warren began to pray for Mark and offer overtures of friendship.

Warren's dad was a dedicated runner who just happened to wear the same size shoes as Mark; the young man accepted the free pair of shoes his new friend offered him. Day after sweaty day, Warren ran beside Mark. Week after week, he let Mark know he cared and that he was willing to listen. Ever so slowly, Mark grew to trust Warren and began to share his struggles and challenges.

Things were tough at home—very tough. Mark's mom had died when he was thirteen. As the eldest of six children, Mark couldn't come to the youth meetings because he had to be home to cook dinner for the whole family. He slept on a mattress in the rafters of the garage. Often Warren didn't know what to say, and he certainly didn't have solutions. But he stayed by Mark's side, took him fishing, listened, and prayed. And when he got the chance, he shared how God came alongside all of us in the person of Jesus. Mark couldn't see Jesus, but he saw his friend and the love he so consistently offered. Mark had already opened his heart to Warren: In time, he opened his heart to Jesus too.

When Mark was in eleventh grade, he was out on his own, working his way through high school. After graduation, he wanted to attend Yuba College. Since Warren and his wife were living in the area, they invited Mark to live with them. A counselor at Yuba College suggested that Mark consider becoming a doctor.

Warren loved Mark, but he didn't think he was the smartest kid on the block. He felt it his duty as a friend to protect Mark from being crushed by the failure that surely awaited him if he aspired to a profession that was above his abilities. He tried to direct Mark toward a trade school where he might be assured greater success than at a highly competitive college. But Mark would not be dissuaded. He believed God had called him to become a doctor. This was awkward for Warren because he wanted to encourage Mark, but he also wanted to be realistic. He'd seen Mark struggle in high school. So Warren did his best to help Mark lower his sights, while still encouraging him to do his very best.

Mark got married and continued his studies at UCLA. It took him seven years to complete his undergraduate work. When he took his test to proceed to medical school, his grades were average. Warren stayed by Mark's side—emotionally and spiritually—and readied himself to help his friend down gently. But that wasn't necessary. What Mark may have lacked in test scores he made up for in character; at least that's what the selection committee said when they admitted him to UCLA medical school.

When Mark became a doctor, no one was more pleased or more proud of him than his longtime friend, Warren. At graduation he received an award as the greatest advocate for humanity in his graduating class. Today, Dr. Mark Knoble has his medical practice in Auburn, California, where he serves as the family physician for Warren Shank and his entire family.

What I find encouraging about this story is that Warren was determined to be a friend because he wanted to make a difference. Even though he knew his limitations from the start, he ventured out to be a friend to one troubled young man. He couldn't run fast, but he was willing to run alongside as best he could.

Warren couldn't solve Mark's problems and often didn't say the right things. He laughingly thanks God that Mark didn't take his shortsighted but well-meaning advice. When I asked Warren about this, he said, "It's definitely contact, not content, that matters most in our friendships." Dr. Knoble was invited to say a few words after Warren shared this story at our church. Mark said, "It's amazing how God works. God takes not ability—but availability. In Warren I see the power of incarnational ministry. We couldn't get to God, so God came to us. There was no way I would have gone to church, so Warren brought church to me. It wasn't what he said, but the relationship—the friendship—that held meaning for me. And what is most amazing is that God works in spite of us."

God used Warren's friendship as a powerful influence in Mark's life when he was going through a difficult time; he helped direct his life on a good course. Warren wasn't the best at being a friend or giving advice or even at running, but he was by Mark's side for the long haul. That connection of friendship made all the difference in the world, to Mark, his family, and all the people who now benefit from his medical care. Warren couldn't make those good things happen, but his willingness to be a friend opened the way for the flow of God's love and power to do exceedingly, abundantly, more than Warren could ask or even imagine for his friend.

What difference can you make? There's no telling what God could do through you if you made yourself available in the same way to someone who's going through hell in your sphere of influence. Bear in mind that it's not a sprint. It's more like a marathon. No wonder we hesitate before signing up for such a race. If you hesitate, remember what we've learned from Warren. You don't have to be the Savior; you only have to be available to the Savior and willing to love your friend with God's help.

THE GREATEST FRIEND THE WORLD HAS EVER SEEN

One cannot consider the obligations of godly friendship without considering the greatest friend the world has ever seen—Jesus Christ. The calling to godly friendship comes not only from the written Word of God but also from the lips of the living Word who became flesh and lived among us. His statements about friendship take on added significance because they were spoken to his small circle of friends on the eve of the greatest act of love and friendship the world has ever seen.

Jesus looked across the supper table into the eyes of the few he called friends in this earthly life and said, "Greater love has no one than this, that he lay down his life for his friends" (John 15:13). At that time, he already knew what he was about to do. We can learn a great deal about godly friendship by watching Jesus with his friends that night. The full account of these events can be found in the Gospel of John, chapters 13 through 21. I will only highlight those passages that relate directly to Jesus' example and commands regarding how we are to treat each other.

Before Jesus told the disciples anything that night, he demonstrated his love by washing their feet. This was the job of the lowliest servant, yet Jesus lowered himself to do this for his friends.

When he had finished washing their feet, he put on his clothes and returned to his place. "Do you understand what I have done for you?" he asked them. "You call me 'Teacher' and 'Lord,' and rightly so, for that is what I am. Now that I, your Lord and Teacher, have washed your feet, you also should wash one another's feet. I have set you an example that you should do as I have done for you. I tell you the truth, no servant is greater than his master, nor is a messenger greater than the one who sent him. Now that you know these things, you will be blessed if you do them." (John 13:12–17)

Note where we find the promise of blessing. We are blessed not for knowing the right thing but for knowing *and doing* the right thing—for serving one another as Jesus has done.

Jesus went on to give what has come to be known as the Great Commandment, the one that sums up all the rest. "A new command I give you: Love one another. As I have loved you, so you must love one another. By this all men will know that you are my disciples, if you love one another" (John 13:34–35).

Apparently, Peter sensed that Jesus was about to go through something difficult. So he asked him, "'Lord, where are you going?' Jesus replied, 'Where I am going, you cannot follow now, but you will follow later.' Peter asked, 'Lord, why can't I follow you now? *I will lay down my life for you*'" (John 13:36–37, italics mine).

Peter made the same impetuous mistake many of us make when we see a friend facing something tremendously difficult. He volunteered to be the hero of the story. But Jesus set him straight.

"Then Jesus answered, 'Will you really lay down your life for me? I tell you the truth, before the rooster crows, you will disown me three times!'" (John 13:38). In essence, Jesus told Peter, "Nope! That's not going to happen. You are not going to lay down your life for me. I am going to lay down my life for you." Jesus knew that even though Peter wanted to run to his rescue, he couldn't pull it off.

Jesus taught his friends many things that night, especially about the source of their life, power, and fruitfulness. They learned that apart from him—in their own strength—they could do nothing. Everything else he said came back to the same main point: Love each other! He repeated this five times that evening (see John 13:34, 13:35, 15:12, 15:17).

Jesus tied their relationships with each other and how they were to treat each other inextricably into their love for him, saying:

"My command is this: Love each other as I have loved you. Greater love has no one than this, that he lay down his life for his friends. You are my friends if you do what I command. I no longer call you servants, because a servant does not know his master's business. Instead, I have called you friends, for everything that I learned from my Father I have made known to you. You did not choose me, but I chose you and appointed you to go and bear fruit—fruit that will last. Then the Father will give you whatever you ask in my name. This is my command: Love each other." (John 15:12–17)

Jesus' promises of joy and a fruitful life are tied to the command that we love each other. No wonder we, as Christians, feel compelled to respond lovingly when we see a friend in need. But this account of Jesus' last night on earth also gives us relief from any sense of inadequacy we may feel regarding our ability to love our friends as Jesus loved us.

Mark's Gospel tells us about how Jesus shared that he was going to be arrested and that all of his friends would abandon him. Then "Peter declared, 'Even if all fall away, I will not'" (14:29). Peter truly believed that his love for Jesus was greater than anyone else's love. He really thought that even though everyone else would fall away, he would not. In his heart, he believed that when push came to shove, he would lay down his life for Jesus. But that's not how the events of the night played out.

Even though Peter's inability to love Jesus to the point of death broke his heart, I thank God that his failure and denial of Jesus are recorded in the Bible. It helps me take heart when what I truly wish I could do for a friend exceeds what I can deliver. I thank God that the point of the story is not that we should summon all our strength and courage to lay down our lives. That would leave us with the obligation to gather enough human strength to get our friends through every trial. And sometimes the challenges and suffering our friends face are more than we can bear in our human frailty.

Rather, this story shows us that when Jesus needed his friends the most, they all turned tail and ran. Even Peter ran away and denied ever knowing Jesus, in spite of loving Jesus as much as was humanly possible and in spite of sincerely believing that he would give his life before he would desert Jesus. It was a human reaction to facing the reality of what Jesus would have to go through.

Even though we would like to think we would do anything for our friends, self-preservation causes us to shy away when they need us most. While it might be hard to admit this about ourselves, realizing that we are not alone in our human tendency to recoil in the face of trouble can give us consolation. It's human nature. Regardless of how much we would love to play the part of the hero in our friends' darkest hours, it is a relief to know that role is reserved for another. It is a relief to know that our human love, our sincere desire to rescue our friends, and our bravest attempts to do so must necessarily fall short.

Jesus is the Savior—not Peter, not me, not you. The One your friends really need is Jesus. When people are going through hell, they need divine love, inexhaustible power, and amazing grace. As much as you wish you could supply these, surely you recognize your limitations. But there is good news! While you are not the Savior, you can be the Savior's vessel through whom he can pour out what your friends need. You are not the Savior, but you can be the Savior's foot soldier, ready to do whatever he commands. You can be the Savior's hard-working farmer who continues to plant good seed in the soil of your friends' hearts, in season and out of season, even when you don't see any growth. You can move as part of the body of Christ to accomplish God's will as your friends go through whatever God allows them to experience.

Jesus said, "Greater love has no one than this, that he lay down his life for his friends" (John 15:13). And Jesus laid down his life. Then he rose from the dead and ascended into heaven, where he is now, seated at the right hand of God the Father. From that exalted position of power, Jesus poured out his Holy Spirit on his followers. He clothed us with power from on high. God is at work within us to will and to do what pleases him—that includes doing our part to help our friends through difficult experiences.

The reality that your friends need more than you can humanly supply is why it is essential to hold on to heaven and your friends. What you wish you could do but can't in your own strength, Jesus can do through you. Jesus can provide, through you, love, power, and wisdom beyond your own limits for situations requiring them. God's divine power can move mountains. God's amazing grace can forgive any sin and redeem any tragic circumstances. Your friends need Jesus. You can be one through whom Jesus ministers to your friends.

You don't have to be the greatest friend in the world to help someone through a difficult time. You just have to stay in close and harmonious contact with the One who is. This works to the degree that you are rightly connected to God and dependent on him. You don't have to be your friends' Savior; just keep running alongside them as you hold on to heaven.

Even though God will help us help our friends who are in trouble, there are reasonable hesitations that come to mind at the thought of venturing into someone else's difficult situation.

For example, my friend, David,* is going through something terribly difficult. I can't shake the sense that there must be something I could do to help, something I *should* do. But I'm not sure what. I care, but I don't know how to show it or whether showing it might obligate me to get more deeply involved than I can be. His situation is complicated, overwhelming. There are no easy answers to his questions. There are no quick fixes.

Besides, I'm not sure I could be of real help to him anyway. The help he seems to need is beyond what I can give. If I reach out to David in his extremity, I don't know where that will lead. To be honest, I'm afraid I

*Not his real name.

don't know what might happen if I get involved in his life as he goes through this. I'm afraid I might fail. I'm afraid he might lash out at me in his frustration and anger. I'm afraid he might latch on to me and expect more than I can give over the long term. Then I would have to pull back and disappoint him. This is something David is going to have to go through. And I'm not sure I am prepared to, willing to, or even supposed to go through this with him.

Looking at my life, I see all my other responsibilities and commitments. I have a family whose needs must rightfully come first. I have a demanding career and deadlines to meet. I have a ministry and a volunteer position at church. All of these internal deliberations lead me to think of Jesus' encounter with a religious expert who asked:

"Teacher, . . . what must I do to inherit eternal life?"

"What is written in the Law?" [Jesus] replied. "How do you read it?"

He answered: "'Love the Lord your God with all your heart and with all your soul and with all your strength and with all your mind'; and, 'Love your neighbor as yourself.'"

"You have answered correctly," Jesus replied. "Do this and you will live."

But he wanted to justify himself, so he asked Jesus, "And who is my neighbor?"

In reply Jesus said: "A man was going down from Jerusalem to Jericho, when he fell into the hands of robbers. They stripped him of his clothes, beat him and went away, leaving him half dead. A priest happened to be going down the same road, and when he saw the man, he passed by on the other side. So too, a Levite, when he came to the place and saw him, passed by on the other side. But a Samaritan, as he traveled, came where the man was; and when he saw him, he took pity on him. He went to him and bandaged his wounds, pouring on oil and wine. Then he put the man on his own donkey, took him to an inn and took care of him. The next day he took out two silver coins and gave them to the innkeeper. 'Look after him,' he said, 'and when I return, I will reimburse you for any extra expense you may have.'

"Which of these three do you think was a neighbor to the man who fell into the hands of robbers?"

The expert in the law replied, "The one who had mercy on him."

Jesus told him, "Go and do likewise." (Luke 10:25–37)

Am I like the pitiless ones who saw a need but passed by because they were too busy doing God's work? I cannot escape the irony of the situation of doing nothing to help my friend because I am too busy writing *Holding on to Heaven While Your Friend Is Going Through Hell*. I cannot escape the still small voice of the Spirit who whispers his name to me whenever I quiet myself in prayer or brings to mind the verses I've memorized: "A friend loves at all times, . . ." (Proverbs 17:17); "A man of many companions may come to ruin, but there is a friend who sticks closer than a brother" (Proverbs 18:24); "Do not forsake your friend . . ." (Proverbs 27:10); "Two are better than one, because they have a good return for their work: If one falls down, his friend can help him up. But pity the man who falls and has no one to help him up!" (Ecclesiastes 4:9–10).

When I say I can't escape these thoughts, I'm admitting that I've tried to. I've thought, *Surely someone else is there for David. Others who live closer are standing by him; they must be.* I let myself off the hook. Then a mutual acquaintance who knows I'm a Christian called me because she was concerned about David. She said he contacted her and confided that he feels as if he has no one. He said that it seems as though everyone has abandoned him. Then she said she prayed and remembered that I have been David's longtime friend.

She mentioned that she had enjoyed hearing me speak at the Women of Faith conference. I wonder if it was her intention to juxtapose the reference to me as a so-called woman of faith with her appeal for me to *do something* to help our friend. Maybe that was all God's doing. I also happened to be going through a Bible study on the book of James at the time. Her appeal called to mind the verses I had studied the night before:

What good is it, my brothers, if a man claims to have faith but has no deeds? Can such faith save him? Suppose a brother or sister is without clothes and daily food. If one of you says to him, "Go, I wish you well; keep warm and well fed," but does nothing about his physical needs, what good is it? In the same way, faith by itself, if it is not accompanied by action, is dead.

But someone will say, "You have faith; I have deeds."

Show me your faith without deeds, and I will show you my faith by what I do. (James 2:14–18)

Her call highlighted my growing sense that—as a Christian and a friend—there must be something God wanted me to do. I thanked her for her concern, and we prayed together for David. When I hung up, I felt convinced that doing nothing was not acceptable.

You probably picked up this book because you have a friend or two in mind who are going through something difficult. Maybe you're wrestling with some of the same issues I've mentioned. Maybe you're hoping this book will help you figure out whether God wants you to do something and what—if anything—you should do. You may be wondering how to help your friends during this time of need and how to do it without having their troubles overwhelm your life. You'll be pleased to know that my reflections on David's needs and my obligation to do something did not leave me baffled. It prompted me to action. And it reaffirmed the validity of the material I have assembled here. I pray and believe it will also help and guide you to help your friends as God would have you do.

I know that standing by while your friends go through difficulties isn't easy. How frustrating to realize that you can't make their problems go away. You cannot reach out and heal an illness with a touch; you cannot wave a magic wand and turn debts into assets; you cannot break the power of sin in someone's life; you cannot make a friend's boss appreciate or promote him or her; you cannot bring someone out of depression, nor can you undo the damage from a terrible childhood, or do a hundred other things you might want to.

While you do not have the power in yourself to do any of these things, God has given you a position of influence. If you are "holding on to heaven," God can flow through you as you remain connected to your friends. Maintain an open and obedient relationship with the living God, and he can show you what to do, give you the power to do it, and guide and help your friends as they go through their trials.

When you see friends going through hell, God can use you as a powerful influence for good. While you don't have to be the Savior, you do have a moral obligation not to turn away. Don't worry that you can't solve their problems or that you might say the wrong things. God can work through you and—when necessary—he can work around you! What matters is that you are willing to run alongside your friends, at whatever pace you can maintain, for the long haul. In the course of time, you will see the special gift of God your friendship has been. And you will be blessed in return.

CHAPTER TWO

Helping Your Friends
When You Feel Powerless to Help

on't worry that you lack the power to help your friends resolve whatever their problems are. People going through hell will always need more than you can humanly give. That's why you need to hold on to heaven. Don't let your lack of power cause you to distance yourself from your friends when they need you most. There is a way to make your point of powerlessness a launching pad from which to enter the flow of God's power, which is all-sufficient. It took a five-year-old to reveal this to my friend Jane.

The past four years have been hell for Jane and her family. The specific details are too shameful and painful to recount for you here; it's enough to say that her world has come crashing down around her. She has lost her marriage, her home, and her job, and has been abandoned by most of her friends.

It's no wonder she felt displaced, devalued, depressed, and discouraged or that she was diagnosed with post traumatic stress disorder. I'll let her tell her story in her own words. Jane wrote,

I left home on December 6, 1998. Needless to say the holiday season wasn't its usual joyous time. I moved into the bedroom of a coworker and his wife. My hope was to accumulate enough money to find a place of my own in a couple of months.

No words can describe the feeling of loss and the depth of loneliness and hurt I experienced the first days. Twenty-six years of marriage and ministry and our family unit were all crumbling. I cried out desperately to anyone who would listen. It felt as though I couldn't make it. I sat in a room by myself and longed to see my own things I had left behind. Eventually I began bringing things from home to my single room, hoping these reminders of the life I left behind might help me feel more at home.

One day I asked my five-year-old granddaughter to spend the night with me. We spent the evening in my room playing, talking, and watching TV. When we were ready for bed, my granddaughter was crawling up to the top bunk. She stopped halfway up the ladder, turned to me, and said, "Grammy, can I pray for you?"

I said, "Sure. What are you praying about?"

She said, "I'm gonna pray for you a house." Then she asked, "What kind do you want?"

I said, "Two bedrooms would be nice; then you could have your own room."

She said, "No, I don't need a bedroom. I'll just sleep with you. This is what we'll ask for: a pool, joyous music, a couch, chair, chips, laundry, a bed, cups, food, and flowers." Then she said, "I'm going to go up to my bunk and pray now." She scurried the rest of the way up the ladder, got down on all fours and prayed, "Dear Jesus, please give my Grammy a house with a pool, joyous music, a couch, chair, chips, laundry, a bed, cups, food, and flowers." Then she added, "You could also give her some soap, lotion, goldfish, milk, candles, Barbies, TV, eggs, hats, a dog, a cat, cheese, pictures, pool toys, homework, a wallet, money, a purse. Oh, yes, and a hair wash. Amen!"

Jane scribbled as fast as she could to get down every word that precious little girl prayed with all her heart on the bunk above her. The next day Jane's granddaughter went home. She called in the afternoon to ask when Jane thought Jesus would have her house ready. She was hoping to go swimming!

How precious! With all that Jane had been through and the overwhelming emotions she was experiencing, we can understand why even concerned friends would shy away. People probably felt powerless to help in the face of such overwhelming heartbreak and complicated family problems. But Jane didn't really need her friends to do anything in particular for her. She didn't expect anyone to fix the things that even she had no power to fix. She just needed friends who would do what her granddaughter did: stay close to her, love her, believe the best for her, and—when they were powerless—turn to the One who is all-powerful on her behalf.

WHEN YOUR FRIENDS' NEEDS ARE BEYOND YOUR POWER TO HELP

Perhaps you already realize that the needs of your friends are beyond your human ability. Maybe you are frustrated in your attempts to help. Perhaps the verses you quote aren't received or your advice falls flat or you don't see evidence that God is hearing, much less answering, your prayers on your friends' behalf. Don't let your frustration lead you to believe that God's Word doesn't work in real life; it does. It just doesn't always work the way we expect it to.

God isn't trying to frustrate you. You may feel as if it's impossible to help your friends through the present issues. But there is a way to accomplish God's will. The life God calls us to is both impossible for us apart from God and entirely possible with God.

Jesus tells us about this kind of life in his parable of the vine and the branches. He said, "'I am the true vine, and my Father is the gardener. . . . Remain in me, and I will remain in you. No branch can bear fruit by itself; it must remain in the vine. Neither can you bear fruit unless you remain in me. I am the vine; you are the branches. If a man remains in me and I in him, he will bear much fruit; apart from me you can do nothing'" (John 15:1, 4–5).

It makes sense that a branch that cannot bear fruit apart from the vine can bear much fruit if it remains connected to the vine. The branch has no other purpose than to bear fruit, but the source of its ability to do so is the vine and the care of the gardener. So, too, those of us who cannot live out some aspect of Christian life have the capacity to do so if we remain rightly connected to Jesus and dependent on our Father in heaven who watches over us. The resources to help your friend, even the wisdom to decide what to do, must flow from this continual dependence on and connection to God.

Use the spiritual principles that follow to check yourself. You may want to share them with your friends so they can apply them as well. As you read this list, notice how Jane's granddaughter did each of these things.

1. Recognize your complete dependence on God.
2. Don't try to manage a situation and control the outcome in your own strength. This only exhausts your energies in fruitless efforts.
3. Direct yourself in developing a closer union with Jesus and trusting in his love and care, even though your heart and mind may waver.
4. Admit and accept things that are impossible for you to change directly. Ask God's direction regarding what you can change, and ask God to take care of what you cannot. It may help to pray the Serenity Prayer often used by AA and other 12-Step groups: "God grant me the serenity to accept the things I cannot change, the courage to change the things I can, and the wisdom to know the difference."
5. Approach God in prayer, praying for what you know is God's will, such as patience and strength to endure. Paul prayed this way for his friends in Colossians 1:11–12: "Being strengthened with all power according to his glorious might so that you may have great endurance and patience, and joyfully giving thanks to the Father..." You may not have faith or even feel led to pray that your friends be

released from their trials, but you can always pray for strength, endurance, and patience.

6. Bring your everyday needs and cares to God. Don't deny your anxiety; instead pass all that makes you anxious on to God in prayer in keeping with 1 Peter 5:7, which says, "Cast all your anxiety on him because he cares for you."

7. Wait and watch for God to fulfill his promises in his own way and his own time.

WHERE ARE YOU?

My goal is to help you remain rightly connected with God so you can respond to your friends and their situations with the love and power of God. To do this, you need to make sure that you are ready to receive the flow of God's power. You may worry because you feel powerless at times. You need to shift from your powerlessness to full dependence on God's power.

Some people recognize from the outset that they are powerless and go directly to trusting God. Others berate themselves for their lack of power and even their lack of faith. They may have tried to believe God's promises, but because they've seen times when those promises seemed to not come true, they doubt. Others think they need great faith to help a friend but don't know how to muster it up—not even faith the size of a mustard seed! They may even feel powerless to overcome their own doubts. There are others who have great human strength, who jump right in with the attitude that they can handle anything, until they find themselves exhausted.

THE POINT OF POWERLESSNESS

All people who want God's power to flow through them must come to a point of powerlessness. It is only when we recognize our weakness, when we discover and admit that a task is impossible, that God's strength can fill our lack.

Here is the simple progression you can make from accepting your powerlessness to receiving God's power by being rightly connected with Jesus. Whenever you hear yourself say, "I can't!" add, "But God can!" Then choose to turn your will and your specific concerns about your friend over to God's care. If you feel responsible for what your friend is going through, turn that over as well.

These are the same principles that begin the 12-Step program used successfully by millions in Alcoholics Anonymous. "(1) Admitted I was *powerless* and my life had become unmanageable. (2) Came to believe that a power greater than myself—whom we know to be Jesus Christ—*could* restore me . . . (3) Made a *decision* to turn my life and my will over to the care of God."[1] This program works because it has tapped into the true application of what Jesus explained in his parable about a branch abiding in the vine.

Understand that realigning yourself to abide in Jesus is not an act of human strength. As a human being, created in the image of God, you have been given the capacity to choose to depend entirely on God. You can do this in any situation, even if your strength has been worn down by stress, heartbreak, or utter exhaustion. It's saying, "God, I can't handle this. I can't control the outcome; I turn it over to your care."

You can use your will to choose to believe God's Word as truth—not just in theory but also in real life. You can choose to turn your life and your friends' lives over to the care of God. This is all done by an act of faith—choosing to believe the best for yourself and your friends and that God's Word is true even if you don't see the good outcome yet. The growth of good fruit takes time and progresses through seasons.

In the parable of the vine and the branches, Jesus told his disciples, "Apart from me you can do nothing" (John 15:5). So, even if all you know is that you feel utterly powerless unless God comes through, that proves part of God's Word. And you can choose to believe that God will bring good fruit as you abide in him and let his words abide in you. The Bible also says, "I can do everything through him who gives me strength" (Philippians 4:13). You can choose to believe that Jesus, the true vine, is sufficient to produce fruit from your life and give you what you will need to be of help to your friends. You can choose to believe that God can work through any situation to cause all things—even bad things—to work together for good, and even bring glory to God and joy out of suffering. But to see the fruit, you have to do what the fruitful branches do; you need to hang in there. Abide.

God is the gardener; and what loving gardener doesn't want to produce good fruit to show off? God wants the fruit of your life to be glorious. Your part is to abide. God the Father will do the work of pruning those who need to be pruned and tending those who need tender care. Jesus is there as the True Vine to strengthen you to help your friends and to sustain your friends as well.

If you want to do something to minister to your friends, don't point out where they are failing to produce the good fruit of love, joy, peace, patience, kindness, goodness, faithfulness, gentleness, and self-control (see Galatians 5:22–23). Instead, encourage them. Remind them that the steadfast love of the Lord never ceases, that nothing can separate them from the love of God. Affirm and reaffirm God's love, mercy, and grace.

Even if your friends have times when they cannot or will not believe God's Word for themselves, keep on believing it for them. If they are Christian, hold on with confidence to the promise "that he who began a good work in you [and your friends] will carry it on to completion until the day of Christ Jesus" (Philippians 1:6). If they are not yet Christian, don't tell them that if they were, they wouldn't be going through this or they would have the benefit of God's comfort. Instead, pray for their salvation and believe that God does not want anyone to perish, but to come to a knowledge of the truth (see 2 Peter 3:9). Then cling to Jesus and keep watching over God's Word to see God make it come true. Remain in this relationship of dependent reliance on God alone. As you are "hanging in there," make use of the promise Jesus gave to those who abide in him and have his Word abiding in them. Ask the Father for whatever you wish and *it shall be done for you!* And be sure to use this promise to pray for your friends.

This isn't a one-time event. It's more like an inner pattern of mind, spirit, and will that you have to practice. If you have the wrong pattern set up as a ritual in your life, you will need to stop yourself anytime you hear yourself say, "I can't!" Remind yourself to add, "But God can! And I choose to turn my life over to him and depend on him entirely to accomplish what I cannot do." How does Romans 12:2 tell us that we are transformed? By the *renewing of our minds*. As you continually renew your mind to agree with God's Word, you will see God transform you. Then you can better deal with your friends and their situations.

The results you hope for friends in pain cannot be forced. Your efforts to make others behave or respond as you want will not help; they will only add stress to your relationship. They may even work against the outcome you would like.

When you come to realize that you are absolutely powerless to make your friends respond as you believe they should or to make God do what you think your friends need, you're in a good spot. You are poised to make the shift from "I can't!" to "God can!" and "I choose to turn my life and my friends over to the care of God." You may have to go through this process repeatedly. But as you continue to redirect your mind and will to choose complete dependence on God, God will take care of the things over which you have no control.

Through your redirection, God can work miraculously in you, in your friends, and in your friends' lives. It takes time; and you probably won't understand exactly how it happens any more than one who watches for grapes to grow on a vine knows exactly how the life of the vine flowing through the branch produces the fruit. You don't need to explain how God can do the impossible. It is enough that you bear good fruit and that you and your friends enjoy it. By this the Father is glorified. Abiding in Jesus is the best thing you can do.

Remember the little girl who prayed such a precious prayer when she had no power to help her grandma? She was heard on high. And she was swimming in the pool at her Grammy's new home and playing Barbies there within a week. (The pool was heated!) Everything she asked and expected God to do for her grandma was done, even though *she* was powerless to make any of it happen. Her prayers even had a direct influence; Jane decided to get a new hairstyle, so even the part about the "hair wash" came true.

CHAPTER THREE

Resting in Confidence That God Will Guide You and Your Friends During Times of Trouble

*J*t can be flattering to have friends look to you for guidance. However, God never meant for you to be the primary means of guidance for your friends—no matter how spiritual you are. The best thing you can do is to guide your friends to God. Then help them learn how to allow God to guide them directly.

It has been said that if you give a man a fish you have fed him for a day, but if you teach a man to fish you have fed him for a lifetime. The same applies to giving guidance. If you give a friend godly guidance for today, you have helped him or her make one decision. You've also made your friend dependent on you, not God. But if you help that friend learn to receive guidance directly from God, you will help him or her make wise decisions throughout life. You will also help to establish a proper relationship with you and with God. It may take time and effort to help your friend learn to receive guidance from God, but in the long run, it is worth it.

No matter how much you love that friend or want to help, you cannot be there all the time. However, Psalm 46:1–3 says, "God is our refuge and strength, an *ever-present* help in trouble. Therefore we will not fear, though the earth give way and the mountains fall into the heart of the sea, though its waters roar and foam and the mountains quake with their surging" (italics mine). The best help you can give your friend is to help him or her get to know and rely on God as an *ever-present* help in times of trouble.

The following section will help you understand the dynamics of this kind of relationship with God and help you explain them to your friend. If you've never experienced this kind of reliance on God for guidance in your own life, perhaps God can use this friend's situation to introduce both of you to a life of dependence on God for tangible help and guidance in times of extremity and adversity.

People going through difficulty will often say things like, "I feel like I'm stuck in the wilderness." They may refer to it as a "wilderness experience." Others just express feelings like these: "I feel so lost!" "I'm so confused; I don't know which way to turn." "This is scary; I can't figure out where God is taking me."

When God has allowed something overwhelming to take your life along an uncharted course, it does feel as if you're wandering in the wilderness. But there is good news. In God's book, the wilderness is the way to the promised land! When God led his people out of slavery, into the good land and good life he promised them, they had to go through the wilderness, and they complained bitterly. They thought God was trying to kill them because of the hardships along the way. However, those hardships were given not to deprive them but to cause them to turn to God, who stood ready to supply all their needs. In this way, God planned to develop their dependence on him and their awareness of his love and power toward them.

You can read the stories of the wilderness journeys of the children of Israel in the book of Numbers. Their experience can hold valuable lessons for any of life's travelers who feel lost or find themselves taking an unrequested detour from the path they wanted to travel in this life. There are several lessons that stand out from the records of the wilderness wanderings of the children of Israel. We see that God was there to provide for them while they were going through extreme times of need. We see that their attitude, their rebellion and disobedience, and their disbelief brought more trouble on them and delayed their arrival in the Promised Land. Even though different people related to God in different ways as they journeyed in the wilderness, God was always available to those who looked to him for guidance.

One key lesson is that our time in the wilderness can be shortened considerably if we take God at his word, expect his guidance, and confidently follow his guidance by faith. By the direct route, it only should have taken the children of Israel eleven days to get through the wilderness on foot (see Deuteronomy 1:2). Instead the whole generation wandered for forty years. And why the delay? The Bible says it was because of their "unfaithfulness"—their lack of faith that God meant what he said and wanted them to apply it in everyday life, specifically with regard to following his guidance in their lives.

Even though they lacked faith, God continued to guide them during their forty years in the wilderness. He kept protecting them and miraculously providing for their needs. But it didn't have to take nearly so long (see Deuteronomy 8:2–9). God is the same today.

One source of frustration people have in times of difficulty is that the problems seem to take them away from their own plans for their lives. We all have plans for our lives. As Christians, we probably consult God in the planning process and try to set our goals within the scope of what we believe to be our callings. When something difficult interrupts those plans, it may threaten to keep us from getting *what we expected* and getting to our goals in the *way we expected* to get there. However, no matter where life takes us, it cannot take us away from God or keep us from receiving his guidance in the process. When we feel as if we are in the wilderness, that is when we should stop following our own plans and diligently follow God's. His plans for our good cannot be thwarted no matter what happens, what we're going through, or where life's turns unexpectedly take us.

The Bible is living and active; it holds truths that come alive in everyday situations. God's promises, combined with your faith, can come alive to help your friends get through their wilderness experiences. One key factor is that they know and *choose* to believe God's promises of guidance that are clearly stated in the Bible. In doing so, your friends can become confident, walk by faith as they go through their wilderness experiences, and be assured that the tender mercies of God are available to meet their daily needs. If you can help others find and believe the Bible promises that apply to their situations, you will help them get through a difficult part of life's journey as quickly as possible.

Consider the following clear promises of God's guidance in the Bible; I suggest you read them over or share them with your friends in pain. Then encourage them to see whether they actually *believe* that these things apply to them. If they have not previously received these promises with faith, encourage them to choose to do so now. Ask, *What would you expect if these promises are true for you in the midst of your current situation?* If a friend hesitates to believe, pray that God will help him or her grasp his promises with a faith that can overcome any unbelief.

- The Bible promises: "If any of you lacks wisdom, he should ask God, who gives generously to all without finding fault, and *it will be given to him.* But when he asks, he must believe and not doubt, because he who doubts is like a wave of the sea, blown and tossed by the wind. That man should not think he will receive anything from the Lord; he is a double-minded man, unstable in all he does" (James 1:5–8, italics mine).

- "Trust in the LORD with all your heart and lean not on your own understanding; in all your ways acknowledge him, and *he will make your paths straight*" (Proverbs 3:5–6, italics mine).

- Jesus said, "My sheep listen to *my voice; I know them,* and *they follow me.* I give them eternal life, and they shall never perish; no one can snatch them out of my hand" (John 10:27–28, italics mine). If you're wondering if this verse applies to believers today with regard to really being able to hear the still small voice of God, consider this: This is the same verse we trust for eternal life. If you apply this as qualifying you to receive eternal life, it follows that you also qualify to *hear his voice* and follow him.

- "Although the Lord gives you the bread of adversity and the water of affliction, your teachers will be hidden no more; with your own eyes you will see them. Whether you turn to the right or to the left, your ears will hear a voice behind you, saying, 'This is the way; walk in it'" (Isaiah 30:20–21).

There are other promises that you may want to search out, but the point is that Christians should expect to receive and be prepared to follow God's guidance. The emphasis of the Old Testament could be summed up as, "Be careful to follow all the commands of the LORD your God, that you may possess this good land and pass it on as an inheritance to your descendants forever" (1 Chronicles 28:8b). However, the emphasis of the New Testament could be summed up in Jesus' call: "Come, *follow me.*" This was not just for the disciples who walked with Jesus on earth, but for all servants of Jesus. He said, "Whoever serves me must *follow me;* and where I am, my servant also will be. My Father will honor the one who serves me" (John 12:26, italics mine). Therefore, we can expect God's personal guidance.

Some people feel uncomfortable with this idea of receiving *personal* guidance from God. Don't let this scare you, even if it is unfamiliar. If this is new for your friends, encourage them to consider the biblical foundation for it and its benefits.

Having the living God as your guide is not cause for fear but for relief from fear. Pastor David George of Valley Springs Presbyterian Church in Roseville, California, tells the following story that exemplifies this truth. He and his family had planned a day of skiing on December 26, 1996. They had made the plans far in advance, invited friends, and looked forward to a brief respite after the busy Christmas season. The day dawned gray and overcast, but they would not be daunted. They headed up to the mountains despite the lousy weather forecast. They arrived at the ski resort to find the parking lot empty and covered with ice. It had been raining, but they were determined to look on the bright side of this drizzly day.

Pastor George suggested that they think of how nice it would be to ski without having to battle the usual crowds. Their attitudes remained undampened, even though their clothing did not. It was sprinkling on the lower slopes, and overall this was not a good day for skiing—no matter how good the skiers' attitudes. They gave it a few hours and made the best of it. Around noon, the group had grown tired of being so cold and wet and wanted to call it a day. Pastor George, and his wife, Jayne, agreed but wanted to make one decent run from a higher elevation before going home. Being confident skiers, they eagerly headed for the ski lift and hopped on. They thought perhaps the weather would be better higher up the mountain.

Not so! The higher they rose, the more the wind whipped at them. They traded in the light drizzle for an icy rain, then for snow flurries, then for heavy snow. As the weather worsened, they looked forward and realized that there were no skiers on the chairs in front of them. They looked back and saw no other skiers on the chairs behind them. As they continued their ascent, the wind swirled the snow so much that they could not see the chair immediately in front of them. That's when the lift stopped—but the winds did not. They hung on to the immobilized lift, dangling there with the wind whipping them about like a toy on a string for twelve long minutes—one wind-whipped second at a time. From this position, their desire to make the best of a less-than-ideal situation seemed foolish. By the time the lift creaked to a start, they had said their prayers and were determined to jump off at the next possible moment.

They approached a platform where it looked possible to make their escape. But a sign stated in big letters: NO EXIT AT THIS POINT. They held on until they reached the top of the lift where they could finally get off. Visibility had deteriorated to the point that they could not tell where they were on the mountain or how to safely get down. And the weather was getting progressively worse. They were chilled to the bone, their clothes and gloves were soaked, and they were scared for their lives.

They decided that their best course of action would be to sidestep down the mountain, hoping to spot a ski patrol. They made their way carefully downward. Eventually they spotted a small shack, which they hoped would be occupied. They made their way to it and were relieved to find a member of the ski patrol inside—dry and relaxed. He assured them that they could easily get down the mountain from there. He drew them a map, showing them that all they needed to do was to go outside, make their way to a clearing, then head downward. They would need to make sure they veered to the right as they passed the first landmark because there was a pretty substantial cliff there, but once they rounded that curve they were home free.

Under different conditions, this wouldn't have been a challenge for either of them; but they had been through a lot. They were not in any emotional or physical condition to just be handed a map and pointed in the right direction. So they asked the man to keep his map and personally guide them down to safety. He kindly obliged, and they gratefully thanked him. Then they followed him down the mountain. When they were reunited with their group, they were more than happy to call it a day. Pastor George used this illustration to explain that when we are in a crisis, we need more than a map from God that tells us general directions. We need a personal guide.

And this is what God does for us. He has supplied the overall map in the Bible of the way we should go. But he also knows there are times when just looking at a map will not be enough—not because of any fault in the map, but because of our own fears and human frailty. There are times we need more than written guidance; we need God to guide us.

The Pharisees were expert "map-readers" of Scripture, but they didn't follow God's guidance. They didn't even recognize Jesus as the promised Messiah, whose coming the Scripture foretold. Jesus told them, ". . . the Father who sent me has himself testified concerning me. You have never heard his voice nor seen his form, nor does his word dwell in you, for you do not believe the one he sent. You diligently study the Scriptures because you think that by them you possess eternal life. These are the Scriptures that testify about me, yet you refuse to come to me to have life" (John 5:37–40).

Another time Jesus told his disciples, "And I will ask the Father, and he will give you another Counselor to be with you forever—the Spirit of truth. The world cannot accept him, because it neither sees him nor knows him. But you know him, for he lives with you and will be in you. I will not leave you as orphans; I will come to you" (John 14:16–18). And again, "All this I have spoken while still with you. But the Counselor, the Holy Spirit, whom the Father will send in my name, will teach you all things and will remind you of everything I have said to you. Peace I leave with you; my peace I give you. I do not give to you as the world gives. Do not let your hearts be troubled and do not be afraid" (John 14:25–27).

Remind friends in difficult situations that—no matter how bad it seems—we do not have to give in to our normal human fears. God is our *ever-present* help in trouble. He is waiting for us to look to him to guide us throughout life, especially in treacherous situations.

We can also rest assured that God intends to guide us to somewhere very good. Keeping this in mind can provide encouragement when the road is rough. Just knowing that God is leading us to safety, leading us somewhere good, can change our attitudes on the journey. Think of how kids approach a trip to an amusement park as compared to somewhere they consider boring. Just knowing that the destination is a good one seems to instill patience and endurance. You can help your friends by reminding them of God's good destination for them.

Sometimes, I think we hesitate to follow God's guidance because we think we know exactly where we want to go in life, and we don't trust that God will take us there. We may be so focused on where *we* want to go that we decide that God's destination would be a disappointment. This misconception keeps us from following God to the best life possible. Those who follow God's leading during times of difficulty may not end up exactly where they expected to go, but God promises to lead them to the plans he has for them. God wants to take us to places far beyond and even better than the limited lives we could imagine for ourselves. However, the road to get there can look anything but promising. That's why it demands our faith in God, not our view of life's passing terrain.

God's Word promises that his intention is to guide our lives toward a good end. When your friends feel confused and unsure of what to do or which way to turn while going through great perplexity, encourage them to take comfort in the promise God sent to the good people of Israel, who were taken captive by their enemies and dragged from their homeland.

God sent this message by the prophet Jeremiah to people in a terrible situation and a terrible place: "'For I know the plans I have for you,' declares the LORD, 'plans to prosper you and not to harm you, plans to give you hope and a future. Then you will call upon me and come and pray to me, and I will listen to you. You will seek me and find me when you seek me with all your heart'" (Jeremiah 29:11–13). Again we have the assurance of a personal relationship and some insight into our destination. We may not know where God is leading us by circumstances beyond our control, but we can be sure that *he knows* where he is taking us, and that his destination is somewhere very good. Perhaps you can help your friends consider how they might respond to God and his guidance differently if they believed this as absolutely true.

Be careful not to act as if it is easy to believe this in the midst of pain or difficulty. Be compassionate. It's hard to believe that God has good plans for you and wants to give you a good future when the hopes you had are threatened or destroyed by a current situation. Be patient. There will be times when the direction your friends' lives take do not make sense. But as part of the process, they will come to realize how a loving God could let them go through it. During the journey, there will be times you will need to help them stretch their faith to believe God's promises. There will also be times when your friends will just need you to stay near until it becomes clear why God has allowed life to take the turns it has taken.

There are times when we won't know where we are going or why we seem to be off course. Only in retrospect will we come to realize that an unwanted detour protected us from dangers we didn't recognize at the time. Something that happened to my husband, Patrick, and me illustrates this. We were returning from Israel in May of 1986. I was very excited by every facet of the experience because our trip to the Holy Land was the fulfillment of a lifelong dream. On the flight home, I studied the map showing the path our plane was scheduled to take as we left the Middle East. I became somewhat confused and concerned when the pilot pointed out landmarks below us that indicated our flight path had diverged from the one shown in the on-board magazine. I anxiously pointed this out to Patrick, but he told me to just relax and enjoy the sights. He assured me that the pilot knew what he was doing.

When we arrived in New York, the television news reported that American military aircraft had received special clearance to take off from Britain to bomb Libya—this was during our confrontation with Muammar Qaddafi. The pilot had diverted our plane around Libyan airspace for our protection but did not announce this change of plans so as not to alarm the passengers.

Looking back on how God has directed our lives, I can see times when God diverted us around dangerous situations. Only when the danger had passed, and we looked back from a position of safety, did we realize God's providential care in what we thought was an unwelcome change of plans. When your friends are concerned and anxious because of unexpected turns in life, you can reassure them that God is guiding their lives even when they don't understand where they're going or why. God remains ever intent on guiding us somewhere good.

While God is always seeking to guide us, we must bear in mind that he respects our free will. Help your friends rest assured that God is watching over their lives and guiding them even when they can't see the larger picture. You can also help them by encouraging them to choose to follow God's leading continually by choosing to obey his Word and follow his leading.

ENCOURAGE YOUR FRIEND TO FOLLOW GOD'S GUIDANCE

There are two ways to experience God's guidance: when he guides us without our knowledge, and when he leads and calls us to follow him. These two often overlap, and are apt to cause some confusion. Our primary goal in the spiritual life should be to remain completely dependent on God, as in the phrases, "I'm just resting in the Lord!" and, "I'm waiting on God to take my life wherever he wants me to go." And while we're in this disposition of complete dependence on God we should also actively seek to do his will. You may be thinking these are contradictory. Which is it—*Should I encourage my friends in need to depend completely on God, or to actively follow God's guidance?* The answer is both—and simultaneously!

Stay with me here. You can understand this concept easily and share it with others so they can also apply it. Picture a friend and his or her current troubles metaphorically, as if that person were approaching a high and rugged mountain range. The destination is on the far side of those mountains, but the mountain range has proven impossible for any human being to scale. Let the mountains represent whatever "hell" your friend is going through. Let the destination represent being where God wants your friend to be in life, accomplishing the things God intends him or her to accomplish and "getting over" whatever mountainous challenges stand in the way.

Some people might be inclined to look at the mountains and conclude that God never meant for them to get over something that immense. Those who are disposed to using all their human strength to obey God's commands would conclude that they had to do their best to try to get over those mountains in their own strength. So they would set out on foot, determined to succeed or die trying. Those who recognize that God wants them to get over the mountains, but that it is also humanly impossible, wouldn't even try to do it in their own strength. They would take one look at the enormity of the mountains before them and begin to search for an airport to see if someone else could fly them over.

The latter response is the one that is completely dependent on God. That response prompts you to go from saying, "I can't!" to, "But God can. Therefore I will turn my life (and my friend's situation) over to the care of God." Turning your life and your friend's situation over to the care of God is done by an act of the will; you simply choose to put yourself and the situation in God's keeping and trust him entirely with the outcome.

You can also encourage your friend to acknowledge complete dependence on God in the same way.

Spiritual dependence on God can be represented by the act of getting into an airplane to fly over the mountains. To help your friend to get over the mountains, you would start by helping him or her trust enough to decide to fly. Flying in an airplane is a matter of choice that you cannot make for someone else, but you can help your friend see that it is the best choice. Once your friend has chosen to fly, he or she would make reservations and, at the appointed time, go to the airport and board the plane. There is no halfway about it! Your friend's life would then be completely dependent on the ability of that airplane to get off the ground and be suspended tens of thousands of feet in the air; if it cannot, your friend's life will be over. You see, it takes faith to board an airplane, but the way one does it is by an act of the will. Just as you could help convince your friend to choose to fly over a mountain range, you can help your friend choose to put his or her faith in God as an act of will to get over the obstacles in the way.

Once your friend gets in that airplane, he or she doesn't have to *do* anything to make sure the aircraft makes it to the destination. The pilot is completely responsible and capable of flying to the appointed destination. Your friend's part is to *get into* the plane and *stay* in.

So let's say that boarding the airplane represents your friend saying yes to God's will in this difficult part of life's journey, becoming completely dependent on God and trusting God wholly—wherever life is headed now. Your friend doesn't have to do anything other than stay committed to God's will and keep believing that God's Word is true, that God really can overcome this and that God intends to help. Your friend's primary part in the deal is to choose to entrust his or her life completely to God throughout the journey.

While entrusting life to God is a matter of the *will*, your friend's *emotions* on this part of the journey are another matter altogether. Some people are relaxed when they fly. Others are nervous wrecks. How they feel about the flight doesn't affect whether they make it to their destination. Their feelings only affect how much they enjoy the ride. Passengers don't even have to carry their own baggage; they can hand it off to some-one before they board if they wish. When the plane experiences turbu-lence, the passengers don't give up and jump out. They sit down and buckle their seatbelts, connecting themselves securely to the plane.

Likewise, God would like his people to trust him enough to turn their lives over to him and simply rest. That is all we need to do. However, if our confidence in the plane or in the pilot is incomplete, we may stay within God's will, but enjoy our "flight" less. As for our baggage, God invites us to cast all our cares and anxieties on him. Any time we feel burdened or weighted down with anxieties, we can hand these cares and worries over to God in prayer. And when we hit turbulence in the form of troubles, the natural response will be to draw closer to God until the troubles pass. This whole idea of being *in Christ* and being completely dependent on God is the basic disposition in which we live the rest of our lives. You may be able to help your friend enjoy this part of the journey more if you can be reas-suring of God's power and ability. You can also help by reminding your friend to cast all anxieties on God because God does care and can help.

Let's take this metaphor to another level. We can agree that although the people in the plane are powerless to keep the plane in the sky, they know that someone can, and they have put their lives completely into the care of the pilot and the plane until they land. In that sense they do not have to *do* anything. They can rest completely. Getting to their destina-tion will happen, without any effort on their parts.

However, once the passengers are in the plane, there comes a time when a voice comes over the intercom and says, "You are now free to move about the cabin." The passengers can then conduct a wide range of activities according to their personal choices. This represents the choices your friend is free to make regarding personal conduct in the midst of these trials, even while his or her primary dependence is placed in God. These are the choices regarding how he or she will *actively seek* and *respond to* God's guidance. The next chapter will show you practical ways to follow God's guidance while continuing to completely depend upon God.

······································
Practical Ways You and Your Friends
Can Follow God's Guidance

*W*hen friends go through hell, they may bring their problems to you, looking for direction. You will need to draw on God's wisdom and guidance to know how to help them. You can also encourage your friends to learn how to follow God's guidance for themselves.

Let's get practical in applying the spiritual understanding of how to rest in the confidence that God is taking care of us, while also making personal choices in keeping with God's guidance. There are a few basics that need to be in operation. We must begin by earnestly desiring God to guide us. We must be looking to follow Jesus and willing to respond to the prompting of conscience and the Holy Spirit, not just trying to follow God's rules and regulations in our own strength.

START WITH SCRIPTURE

We must always start with God's written Word, even though we're trusting the living Jesus who abides in us to empower us to keep it. All our basic decisions can be influenced by the principles given in the Bible. Therefore, we need to have a good understanding of what God's Word

················

says. This can be intimidating. The Bible consists of sixty-six books, some of which you or your friends may not have read or fully understood. So how can you be confident that the principles that guide your decisions are in keeping with the whole of Scripture?

There is an easy way. Jesus always did the will of the Father. Jesus kept the law on every point. So we don't have to wait until we can comprehend the whole of Scripture to start testing our decisions by it. All we have to do to make a good start is to get to know Jesus. This is something you could help your friends do if they are seeking to grow in their understanding of how to follow God. If your friends know what Jesus is like—and they can by undertaking a prayerful reading of the four Gospels, or even just the Gospel of John—they can have a guide to follow in making decisions.

This form of basic decision making has been popularized in the book *In His Steps* by Charles Sheldon and more recently in a youth edition of the same book. The premise is that an entire town was revolutionized by obeying the simple idea that Jesus has left us an example, and we should follow in his steps. The characters in a fictional town were challenged to ask themselves one question—"What would Jesus do?"—before making any decision, then to follow through and do whatever the answer dictated.

This rule of guidance is so simple and profound that its application has transformed lives and is now sweeping through the youth culture. "WWJD?"—seen on T-shirts and jewelry—reminds kids how to let God guide them every day and in every way by asking, *What would Jesus do?*

The other basic rule of scriptural guidance is the rule of love. This is summed up in the Golden Rule, as Jesus said, "'Love the Lord your God with all your heart and with all your soul and with all your mind.' This is the first and greatest commandment. And the second is like it: 'Love your neighbor as yourself.' All the Law and the Prophets hang on these two commandments" (Matthew 22:37–40).

Paul also affirmed this in greater detail in his letter to the Romans, "Let no debt remain outstanding, except the continuing debt to love one another, for he who loves his fellowman has fulfilled the law. The commandments, 'Do not commit adultery,' 'Do not murder,' 'Do not steal,'

'Do not covet,' and whatever other commandment there may be, are summed up in this one rule: 'Love your neighbor as yourself.' Love does no harm to its neighbor. Therefore love is the fulfillment of the law" (Romans 13:8–10). So whenever your friends have decisions to make, encourage them to start by asking, "What would Jesus do?" Then check all actions by the Golden Rule.

LOOK FOR PRACTICAL ADVICE IN THE BIBLE AND APPLY IT

Next, encourage your friends to find any practical advice the Bible offers regarding the issues associated with the kinds of decisions they must make. The Bible is full of practical advice and detailed instruction on the most important basic aspects of life. If they don't know how, teach your friends how to use a good concordance (which lists key words and points out where they are in the Bible) or a study Bible that leads from topic to topic. The instruction in God's Word is given to teach us, to help us see when we are out of line, to correct us, and to train us to live the kind of lives God intends, so that we "may be thoroughly equipped for every good work" (2 Timothy 3:17b). This is a rich source of sound guidance from the One who made us and knows how we should live.

I came to appreciate this more fully when I wrote a series of self-help books on family roles. One focused on how to be a great wife and another on how to be a great husband. The premise was to show people how to apply biblical principles in marriage. As we directed the books to a general audience, however, I simply explained how to set goals to do what God says we should without quoting Scripture and verse. It was basic Bible application to everyday life.

I later received a call from a woman who could not find these books in stock in her area. She was a dorm mom at the University of Texas and wanted the books to give as wedding gifts to young couples. In our conversation, she commented about how much wisdom there was in what I had written, and she asked how I had gained such wisdom. When I told her that all I'd done was apply what the Bible says, she was shocked. She said she was an atheist and had no idea that the Bible contained such effective advice for everyday life. Her comments made me realize that we often take for granted the riches of wisdom we have at our fingertips when we have the Bible within reach.

WALK IN THE LIGHT YOU HAVE

Once your friends have a sense of what is right and what the Bible says specifically about their situations, it's time to begin obeying what the Bible says. Knowing what to do is one thing; carrying it out is another. How do we manage to obey God's guidance in Scripture? One step at a time. Psalm 119:105 says, "Your word is a lamp to my feet and a light for my path." This imagery comes from ancient Palestine, where shepherds had to keep watch over their flocks day and night. Many dangers could lie underfoot, so they needed a form of illumination to walk in the dark. At night they strapped lamps to their ankles; that way, when they walked, they had light for the path.

David wrote here that God's Word does the same thing for us. God's Word does not promise to illuminate the entire journey all at once, but it will illuminate the next step. That step must be taken by faith. When your friends must make decisions regarding present circumstances, God's Word will give them enough illumination to know which steps to take. This is how we "walk by faith" in practice.

Have your friends ask themselves, "Is there one step that I could take now that is clear from God's Word?" If there is, encourage them to ask the Lord to give them the grace, courage, and strength to take that step. So we walk in the light we have, and God will give more light for each step. Remind your friends not to get ahead of themselves and not to hesitate to take the step that is clearly right just because they don't know what might follow.

CONTINUE TAKING SPIRITUAL AND PRACTICAL STEPS

God doesn't want us to wait for his advice for every step we take any more than he wants your friends to ask your advice for every step they should take! God gave us his written Word, the Bible, as guidance. He also gave us intelligence and free will. God expects us to use all three! None of us needs God to tell us personally to forgive someone. That's a given in the Bible. Any time God's Word + common sense = a specific action, we should not expect God to give us some supernatural "leading" or special revelation. God always leads us to forgive; that is indisputable in the Bible. It is our responsibility to seek God for the grace to continually walk in that. The same holds true for many other issues where Scripture clearly tells us what we should do.

We must also be careful not to misuse Scripture by taking an isolated verse or part of a verse out of context and using the words to support an action that is contrary to the whole of God's Word. We can easily deceive ourselves, especially when we want something that contradicts God's Word. Therefore, you can help your friends stay on the right track by showing them how to test their take on any isolated verse with WWJD?, the Golden Rule, other Bible verses, and other beliefs accepted as orthodox Christian doctrine. *Never* decide to go against Scripture because of some inner impression or supernatural "revelation." Impressions, spiritual influence, and even supernatural phenomena can come from sources other than God. If the spiritual influence is of God and the Holy Spirit, it will *never* contradict the Bible. For example, God will never tell you by an inward impression to break one of the Ten Commandments—however, your own heart might.

INWARD IMPRESSIONS

There are two common extreme responses to inward impressions as they relate to receiving God's guidance. One is to dismiss them out of hand, and the other is to rely on them entirely. Those who dismiss them are missing out on one of the most beautiful privileges of walking with our living Lord Jesus Christ. Those who rely on them entirely risk going off into heretical teachings; they also risk becoming immobilized in their Christian walks while waiting for "a word from the Lord." God expects us to continue walking in his Spirit by exercising the free will and common sense he gave us to go with his written Word.

The New Testament church teaches and exemplifies a healthy balance between walking by faith while using our God-given freedom of choice and being responsive to the inner witness of the Holy Spirit as it speaks to us. Let me explain how to help your friends keep this balance while enjoying the freedom God has given all his children.

Look at the life of the apostle Paul. After his miraculous conversion, he had no doubt that God certainly could speak to him. He knew God could stop him dead in his tracks and knock him off his horse if he had good reason to do so! But Paul didn't allow his spiritual life to become immobilized while he waited for miraculous revelations from God every day. He was a faithful member of his local church in Antioch, where he was one of the leaders. "While they were worshiping the Lord and fasting, the Holy Spirit said, 'Set apart for me Barnabas and Saul for the work to which I have called them.' So after they had fasted and prayed, they placed their hands on them and sent them off. The two of them, sent on their way by the Holy Spirit, went down to Seleucia and sailed from there to Cyprus" (Acts 13:2–4). Paul knew what his calling was, what his gifts were, and what he wanted to do. He operated within a community of faith where his friends and church leaders partnered with him in prayer and the pursuit of God's will—as you can do with your friends. Paul went where the Holy Spirit sent him, but he also had goals and desires that influenced his decisions. Notice in the following passage how Paul was moving in the direction God had given him and setting his course as he thought best. Yet he remained ready to change his course when God intervened to give him specific direction.

Paul and his companions traveled throughout the region of Phrygia and Galatia, *having been kept by the Holy Spirit from preaching* the word in the province of Asia. When they came to the border of Mysia, *they tried to enter* Bithynia, but the Spirit of Jesus *would not allow them to.* So they passed by Mysia and went down to Troas. During the night Paul had a vision of a man of Macedonia standing and begging him, "Come over to Macedonia and help us." After Paul had seen the vision, we got ready at once to leave for Macedonia, concluding that God had called us to preach the gospel to them. (Acts 16:6–10, italics mine)

This is a beautiful picture of active trust in God's guidance. Paul felt free to proceed in what he knew God had called him to do. Because he was in close fellowship with the Lord, Paul trusted that God would redirect him if he started to go the wrong direction. Or God could get a message to him regarding where he was to go. Part of your ministry to friends going through difficulty can be to encourage and help them to develop this level of trust and intimate relationship with God. However, there is one thing you must remember and perhaps remind your friends about. This kind of guidance only works when we are completely willing to go wherever the Lord tells us to go and do whatever he tells us to do. This can be scary to people who have never fully surrendered their lives to God, but once they experience this kind of adventurous faith life, they'll never want to live any other way!

Here's what this means for your friends: They are free to set goals and move out in any direction, as long as they stay within God's moral will. Encourage them to pursue the specific calling God has put on their lives (to whatever degree they know what that is). They should remain open to hear what God might say—through an inner impression, a verse of Scripture, a dream, a word of encouragement or correction from other Christians, or other supernatural means. They should always test the spiritual source by comparing any guidance received to what is clearly written in the Bible (and you may be called on to help with this if you know more about the Bible). Any time they believe God is impressing them to do something that is in keeping with God's Word and would hurt no one, even if they're not sure it's "from the Lord," they can feel free to move ahead. What could it hurt to do what the Bible says?

When your friends move out in the directions they *think* God wants them to go—whatever the source of that inspiration—encourage them to look to providential circumstances. God can guide or he can stop your friends by circumstances. God was able to stop Paul and his companions as they sought to enter Bithynia. If God wants your friends to go somewhere else or do something else, he can use circumstances or other means to direct them.

However, if a friend feels "led of the Lord" to do a certain thing or to pursue a certain course of action, a "closed door" or adverse circumstances doesn't always mean it is not God's will. It may be that he or she is experiencing opposition from the spiritual forces of wickedness that continually try to thwart God's plans. God can handle them! If that friend feels led of God, tries to follow that leading, and can't do it—but the inner desire persists—encourage him or her to pray that God will overcome any spiritual resistance that may be interfering with his will. Then your friend can trust that God is in control. God can easily change the circumstances so your friend can accomplish what is in his or her heart.

Encourage that friend to patiently trust God. It might be that God is prompting him or her in a particular direction for the purpose of prayer, but that the time for the fulfillment of what God is calling for will come later. If a leading is truly from God, he will make a way for it to be accomplished in his time. Romans 12:12 tells us, "Be joyful in hope, patient in affliction, faithful in prayer." But we don't like to be patient in affliction. We like to get out of affliction immediately. The natural human desire to get out of pain, even if it means disobeying God's Word, can cause your friend to think God is pointing the way to a shortcut, a quick fix that will numb the pain. Your friend may try to justify using drugs or other mood-altering substances or taking part in other wrong activities to ease the pain. He or she may become convinced that God condones an illicit sexual relationship because the "right" person came along—while ignoring or justifying the fact that the "right" person is married to someone else. The mind plays strange tricks on us when we are going through life's difficulties. Part of your role will be to help this friend learn patience and to resist believing that God leads us to do anything that goes against the teachings of the Bible.

If you can help your friends patiently endure whatever they must as they seek God's guidance, a time will come when they can experience the most beautiful aspect of God's guidance. When we are fully committed to letting God guide our lives, he guides us by the desires of our hearts, even though the unyielded heart is deceitful and will lead us astray. The yielded heart, where Jesus abides, is changed so that our desires, the deepest longings of our hearts, spring from the heart of God himself. He causes us to desire inwardly the very thing he wants to bless us with outwardly. Then as we eagerly pray for and pursue the desires of our hearts, God delights to lead us to the fulfillment of what we most desire.

The Bible says that God is at work within us both to will and to do of his good pleasure. When we are living in this kind of close relationship with God, looking to him for guidance and actively following it, David's prayer applies to us: "May he give you the desire of your heart and make all your plans succeed" (Psalm 20:4). God can gladly make all our plans succeed, because our plans have been inspired by the Spirit of God working in us and flowing through us. Encourage friends in difficult situations to pursue this kind of intimate relationship with God. Then you will not only help them through this rough passage of life, but you will also help them to fulfill God's purpose for their lives. What joy it is to live this way, even when—or perhaps, especially when—friends are going through hell. If they learn to practice following God's guidance, trusting that he will guide them, indeed *is guiding* them even when they don't know it, and trusting that God intends to guide them to a good place, your friends can find solace even in an arduous part of life's journey! If you trust God to guide you as you seek to help your friends, you can rest assured that God will lead you, even when you are not sure which way to turn.

Next we will look at various aspects of friendship and what it means to be a friend when someone is going through extreme times.

CHAPTER FIVE

To Befriend Is an Action.
Do It!

*I*t has been said that "a friend is the one who comes in when the whole world has gone out." When someone you know is going through hell, the validity of your friendship will be determined not so much by sentiment or what you say, but by your actions. First John 3:18 says this: "Dear children, let us not love with words or tongue but with actions and in truth."

One friend of mine, Annette,* has been "going through hell" for the past four years. Before her crisis, she and her husband had pastored a church together in a tight-knit denomination for fifteen years. Annette participated in women's ministries within her denomination. Over the years, she developed a friendly camaraderie with other pastors' wives and had come to consider many of them her friends as well as ministry associates and sisters in Christ. Back then, most of them would probably have called Annette a friend.

Then charges were brought against Annette's husband, accusations that he had been sexually involved with a minor in their congregation. The charges proved true; police arrested him, he pleaded guilty, and the news media descended on Annette's entire family. A lawsuit was brought

*Not her real name.

against the church, the denomination, Annette and her husband, and a fellow staff member of the church.

If ever Annette needed her friends, the time had come. But this was such a difficult set of circumstances. Rumors circulated that perhaps she had known, even though she had not. People suggested that perhaps she had not been able to fulfill her "wifely duty" because she had been sick the previous year. Hmmm . . . were they blaming her for her husband's behavior? How does one talk about such things? And Annette's defense against the overwhelming shame and pain was to find solace in her sense of humor. Some said she was behaving inappropriately by joking around when she should have been somber.

Annette found herself out of work—it's hard to be the pastor's wife when he's serving time as a sex offender. She was financially devastated by the legal costs and the loss of their income. She took a menial job in a cafeteria in a Christian setting where many of the women who had been her peers came for lunch. When she served them, most of them averted their eyes or made little real contact with her. Because of the ongoing lawsuit against the denomination, its headquarters followed policy and asked those still employed not to make contact with anyone else being sued. That meant that Annette's primary associates from the past fifteen years were restricted from contacting her. One women's ministry leader did call her in spite of the ban, but none of Annette's other "old friends" called.

Annette stood by her husband during the trial and eighteen months in jail. After his release, she tried to help him reestablish his life. This was extremely difficult because they had lost their home, all their nice possessions, their reputations, and almost all of their friends. They worked together to try to repair the damage to their lives. When their counselor outlined how much emotional work they would need to do, what they would need to rehash and work through to resolve the pain of the present and the residue of the past, Annette's husband finally gave up. He didn't want her to have to go through so much with so little promise of a payoff. Even though he still loved her and she still loved him, he suggested that they might be better off if they separated.

Annette had promised herself and her husband that if he ever suggested a marital separation or divorce—even after all she had been through with him—she would grant it, even though it broke her heart. Annette called me several months after she and her husband had decided to separate. Her family and some people at her new job knew, but she had been too ashamed to tell anyone else. I listened to her and prayed as to how I could befriend her at this time. I realized that she needed the support of her Christian friends, but she had become estranged from them. I asked if I could call a woman who was well connected in her previous denomination, one who did not personally know Annette but was associated with her old friends. Annette agreed that I could call her.

When I called and explained the situation, the woman I'll call Judy agreed to meet Annette and me for dinner. When Annette poured out her whole story, Judy expressed concern and her apologies on behalf of the women who had let Annette down when she needed them most. Then Judy invited us to attend a regional gathering of the denomination's women's ministries. Annette was hesitant, but she knew that she needed the support of a circle of friends. She also knew in her heart that none of those women meant to harm her by their absence in her life.

When Annette attended the gathering, it had been at least four years since she had seen most of the women there. Many did a double take before registering who she was and how they knew her. Over and over again she was asked, "How are you?" "How have you been?" "What has happened to you?" Each woman expressed kindness and concern and was saddened and taken aback to learn that no one from the association had kept in touch with Annette when she was going through such deep waters. There were many apologies and promises to keep in touch.

I don't share this story to berate that particular group of women. On the contrary, I chose that group of women because I know them to be especially loving and sincere Christians. It's just that human nature took over. When disaster strikes, especially when it is so complicated and messy, people tend to assume that someone else is *surely* there for those in pain. We would do better to assume that everyone will assume that someone else is going to be there while they themselves shy away. These women are in good biblical company. Most of David's friends abandoned him. Most of Job's friends turned their backs or worse—made fun of him and spit on him. The friends who did stay by Job's side blamed him for his own misfortune. Even Jesus' friends scattered when his night of agony came. So let's not be too hard on ourselves when we hope someone else will step in to befriend someone in times of extreme difficulty.

However, if you are going to be a real friend, you must *befriend* the one going through difficulty. *Befriend* is a verb—an action word. It means you are one of the people who goes into a friend's life when the world goes out. It means you won't just say you care; you'll do something.

One of the saddest comments I heard in the aftermath of the killings at Columbine High School was made by a girl who considered herself somewhat a friend of Dylan Klebold. As she walked along the hillside where the crosses and makeshift memorials stood in silent tribute to those Dylan and Eric Harris had killed, she said, "Dylan had friends other than Eric. I guess he just didn't know he had friends." Those of us who consider ourselves a friend to someone who is troubled need to express our friendship overtly, while we have the chance. How sad to think that someone who apparently keenly felt the absence of friendship turned his anger, vengeance, and pain into terrible deeds that left a nation in tears. This is not to say that anyone other than the killers are guilty of the crimes. However, if we can learn from this experience to be more expressive of our caring, let us not lose the opportunity to bring some small measure of good out of something evil.

WHAT SHALL I DO?

When friends are going through extreme difficulty, you probably won't know what to do—exactly. The more difficult the situation, the more perplexed you may feel as to what would be appropriate for you to do. However, the remedy to not knowing what to do is *not* to do nothing. There are many things you can do. You don't have to do them all, but choosing to do something—even if it seems a tiny thing—is far better than failing to do anything because you're not sure what to do.

Start by following the old adage, "Find a need and fill it." I interviewed a mother and daughter who had lost the husband/father of their family to cancer three years earlier. As they told me all the ways that friends had pitched in to help, their eyes shone with tears of gratitude. They told of those who sent cards, letters, and words of sympathy; those who had come to sit with them at the hospital or to spend the night after he passed away.

The daughter was about to begin college when her father died and wavered in her decision to leave home. One of her father's friends talked to her the way he thought her father would have at such a time. She went on to college in southern California. When the teachers were hard on her, not realizing the grief she was going through at the time, another of her father's friends flew down to the college and met with her professors to help them understand the stress she was under so they would be some-what more accommodating and not misjudge her. Other friends of the family realized that she probably wasn't having much fun, being away from home immediately after losing her father, so they bought her a year-round pass to Disneyland. They figured she could find some respite from her sorrow at the "Happiest Place on Earth."

The wife/mother of the family told me how friends had helped her learn to deal with the business and financial concerns she had to address. One friend had the foresight to realize that she would need something to look forward to, so this friend promised to take her somewhere special once each month. Sometimes they went to the theater or out to a nice dinner and a movie; but what really mattered was that she had something special to look forward to from month to month.

Their friends pitched in to help in a variety of ways. Most of the help came because a friend recognized a need by looking at the situation and applying the Golden Rule. They asked themselves, "What would I want someone to do for me if I were in that situation?" Then they did or offered to do whatever they thought would help. If you are at a loss for practical ways to encourage or help a hurting friend, I recommend the little book *Stand By Me* by Dave and Jan Dravecky.

The list that follows includes several categories of things you can do to be of help to friends in times of trouble. Each category may have various levels of involvement. Only do what you can handle within the limitations of your life, but do something. I suggest you pray and ask the Holy Spirit to lead you to see the unmet needs and how you can help fill them.

- *Call yourself a friend.* When trouble strikes, you will begin to see people aligning themselves on various sides of the issues involved. You can make it known publicly that you still consider your friends a part of your life and that you intend to stand by them. You don't have to approve of all that your friends may have done; you don't have to even know all the details of what is going on. You can make it known publicly that no matter what, you intend to remain a faithful friend.

- *Reaffirm your love.* When our family went through a severe crisis a decade ago, there was tremendous shame associated it. We were afraid that people had turned against us, but we were too afraid of further rejection and too ashamed to take a poll of our former friends to see who still claimed to love us. We simply waited. Over the course of time, our true friends reached out to us to let us know they still loved us. Those who did not drifted away and we came to view them as former friends or wondered if they had ever truly been friends. The reaffirmation of love offered us by those who stood by us during our shame and suffering was priceless. Some could do nothing more, but their reaffirmation of love meant so much to us at the time that they didn't need to do more.

- *Just listen.* We underestimate the value of listening when someone we care about is hurting or going through something difficult. I think of the time when Jesus visited Martha and Mary's home for dinner. Martha scurried about, while Mary sat at Jesus' feet—just listening to him. When Martha complained that Mary wasn't helping her make preparations, Jesus said that Mary had chosen "the best part" and that he wouldn't take that away from her. Granted, "the best part" Jesus referred to was that Mary was listening *to him*. However, this can serve to remind us that sometimes the best we can do for hurting friends is not to scurry about trying to do something physical. Sometimes the best part is to just listen—attentively and without distractions.

Here are some tips on "just listening" for you to follow:

1. *No cross talk*. This is a rule at all Alcoholic's Anonymous and 12-Step meetings that works wonderfully. It means that when someone else is talking, you don't interrupt. You can nod or make eye contact, but let your friend talk until he or she stops.

2. *Keep what you hear absolutely confidential*. This is another great rule of communication that makes AA so successful. If your friend shares anything with you, keep it in the strictest confidence. If you have some need to share it with another, perhaps to get further help, always get specific permission first and tell your friend what you intend to say. You may find that your interpretation of what you think you heard is incorrect.

3. *Show your empathy*. Don't be afraid to share in a friend's emotions. The Bible teaches us to weep with those who weep and rejoice with those who rejoice. You can also express indignation when you hear of injustice or share anger at what has caused harm. Let your friend know that you have heard and you care.

• Participate in a circle of friends or a support group. The best biblical example of an effective support group I can think of can be seen in the story related in Mark's Gospel.

> Some men came, bringing to him [Jesus] a paralytic, carried by four of them. Since they could not get him to Jesus because of the crowd, they made an opening in the roof above Jesus and, after digging through it, lowered the mat the paralyzed man was lying on. When Jesus saw their faith, he said to the paralytic, "Son, your sins are forgiven."
> Now some teachers of the law were sitting there, thinking to

themselves, "Why does this fellow talk like that? He's blaspheming! Who can forgive sins but God alone?"

Immediately Jesus knew in his spirit that this was what they were thinking in their hearts, and he said to them, "Why are you thinking these things? Which is easier: to say to the paralytic, 'Your sins are forgiven,' or to say, 'Get up, take your mat and walk'? But that you may know that the Son of Man has authority on earth to forgive sins . . . ." He said to the paralytic, "I tell you, get up, take your mat and go home." He got up, took his mat and walked out in full view of them all. This amazed everyone and they praised God, saying, "We have never seen anything like this!" (Mark 2:3–12)

This man had two major problems: He was paralyzed, and he was struggling with real moral guilt over his sins. His friends were powerless to change either of these conditions. However, someone heard that Jesus was in town. They figured that Jesus could do something to help, but no single friend could have gotten the paralytic man to Jesus. It took four of them to carry him, and a whole group of friends came along. The Bible doesn't detail their preparations, but surely someone had to come up with the idea of how to get past the obstacles keeping the man from the help he needed. Someone had to find the way up onto the roof. Several had to dig through the roof. Someone had to design a device so they could lower the man through the hole in the roof without dropping him. This had to be a group effort.

The same is true of your friend's need while he or she goes through difficulty. No one person will be able to do everything necessary in the prolonged process of getting through this. And truly, you and your other friends must realize that God is the only One who has the power to remedy the situation. However, you can align yourself with others who also care about your friend. Together, you can address the problems as they arise. You can figure out how to bring this person "before the Lord." You can pool your resources, strengths, and ingenuity to overcome obstacles as they arise. You can encourage each other to do what perhaps none of you would dare to do on your own.

When it comes to helping a friend through trouble, you don't have to do it all. You don't have to do it alone. You don't even have to carry a heavier load than you can bear. You can work with others to create an ongoing support group. Here is some practical advice on being part of such a support system.

1. *Make sure that no one becomes overwhelmed or exhausted.* It is common for close friends and family members to exhaust themselves when someone they love is going through something extremely difficult. You can help each other by being on the alert for signs of exhaustion in each other. When exhaustion sets in, it's time to offer some relief or to enlist more help.

2. *Meet with others who want to help to organize what each person will do.* Focus on having people do what they do well, want to do, enjoy, and/or are gifted to do. When we went through our crisis, certain people became our primary emotional support and we confided in them our thoughts and feelings. Others helped primarily in practical ways. A few seemed appointed just to pray or listen when I needed to talk. These people all kept in touch with each other to encourage each other and discuss our changing needs for support.

3. *Realize that different needs arise in different stages of the process.* If someone's life changes so that the help he or she originally offered is no longer tenable, make adjustments as a group. Look for fresh recruits to take up some of the slack. Give each other times for refreshment and encourage each other to rest when necessary.

4. *Recognize the various kinds of support that are needed.* Let each person fit where he or she naturally fits best or where each one's spiritual gifts can be best used. Support can be practical: providing physical help, meals, or financial support; helping to organize and delegate responsibilities; doing housework; or taking on duties that your friend can't handle. Support can be emotional: weeping when your friend weeps, finding ways to create laughter or lift spirits, listening without

condemnation, being kind and tenderhearted. Support can also be spiritual: praying, giving godly counsel, providing guidance to portions of the Bible that may answer particular questions. Each area of support is important.

5. *When the support group is faced with a problem you can't solve or a need you can't fill, don't pretend that you can.* Instead, have someone do the research to find out who can help and how to reach those persons or organizations, then reach beyond your support circle to get the help that is beyond you—whether that help is from people, organizations, or God.

There is no substitute for the love of faithful friends who are willing to do whatever they can to help in times of need. Whatever you do, whatever you realistically have to offer, I hope you will make sure to *befriend* those in need in some tangible way. There is a good return for such labor. I know because I can trace every book I have written and every bit of the ministry that has flown from my life after our family crisis back to the love and faithfulness of those who carried us through it. Not all of them had a great deal of time or money or even practical help that they could offer us. They had their own families and responsibilities; but every one who declared that he or she was still our friend played a part in getting us through a terrible crisis. Without that love and support, you would not be reading this book today because I would not have been able to write it.

Just as this book and many other good things came as a result of our friends' willingness to come in when all the world was going out, so too will your willingness to befriend others bring good rewards. You will see in days and years to come that you will receive a good return for whatever labor is involved in carrying your friends along in times of need. God bless you for all that you do for your friends when they need it most!

A CIRCLE OF FRIENDS

The whole idea of being part of a circle of friends is magnetic. Who doesn't want to belong? Who hasn't known the pain of standing on the sidelines alone watching a tight-knit circle of friends have fun together? Any kinder-gartner can tell you all about it. Any junior high kid can tell you about the fear of being the last one picked for a team. Any high school student can tell you about the fear of not having a group to sit with at lunch. But it doesn't stop there. Ask the middle-aged divorcé or divorcée what it's like to walk back into church alone, hoping someone will reach out. Every one of us, at every phase of life, longs to be welcomed into a circle of friends.

That's the catch, we must be welcomed in; when we enjoy being part of a circle of friends, we need to be aware and reach out. In 1998 I trav-eled with the Women of Faith "Bring Back the Joy" tour, which featured six women speakers and the musical group Point of Grace, whose song "Circle of Friends" topped the charts at the time. I participated in half of the conferences as a guest speaker. At the opening of each conference, a video showed the six featured speakers enjoying each other's company—praying together, playing together, weeping and laughing together—all to the music of "Circle of Friends."

The idea was to encourage the thousands of women in these huge arenas to come together as a circle of friends and celebrate. But as I sat in the audience, I often looked at the faces of the women around me as they watched the video. I became aware that some of them were not sharing in the joyous celebration. When the lyrics talked about trying to fit in, I could almost pick out the ones who were still trying. Many times I felt led to pray for those who did not have a particular circle of friends in which they felt welcomed.

In keeping with the theme of modeling a circle of friends, the six fea-tured speakers sat together on a small porch directly off stage. As Point of Grace sang the song, they called the "circle of friends" up on stage to join in on the chorus. As a guest speaker, I was usually seated in the audi-ence, not on the porch. However, at one conference, one of the featured speakers was absent, so I was seated on the porch with the other ladies. An awkward moment arose when the featured speakers were called up on stage to join hands in the "circle of friends." The others rose to join Point of Grace as they always did, but I stood frozen. There was no way

I was going to risk including myself in this part of the program, but neither did I want to stand alone on the porch. I was keenly aware that I needed someone to help me out of this potentially embarrassing moment. Denise Jones, one of the members of Point of Grace, locked eyes with me. I don't think she knew what we were supposed to do either. But she reached out her hand to me, smiled, and called me into the circle of friends.

Her smile and outstretched hand was such a relief in that awkward moment. It has come to be a symbol for me, one I share with you. When you are happily part of any circle of friends, it's fine to celebrate and enjoy the blessings of belonging. But don't let the blessings stop there. Look around to see if there are others nearby, awkwardly wondering if anyone has noticed that they aren't part of your circle. They aren't going to risk trying to join you unless you invite them in. The risk you take in including them is far less. Befriend them. Make eye contact. Smile. Reach out your hand. Bring them in to the shelter of your circle of friends.

....

CHAPTER SIX

Being a Godly Friend:
The Qualities of a Good Friend That Make a Difference

T here is another perspective we can have on the idea of befriending someone who's going through difficulty. That is to put the emphasis on the *being* part of *befriend*.

Henri Nouwen captured the aspect of being a friend when he wrote: "A friend is that other person with whom we can share our solitude, our silence, and our prayer. A friend is that other person with whom we can look at a tree and say, 'Isn't that beautiful,' or sit on the beach and silently watch the sun disappear under the horizon. With a friend we don't have to say or do something special. With a friend we can be still and know that God is there with both of us."[1]

One of the greatest aspects of being a true friend when someone is suffering is that you can just be together without having to talk about everything or even having to do anything. It's a matter of being friends.

QUALITIES OF LOVE

The added dimension of holding on to heaven or being a Christian should influence the kind of friend you will be. Proverbs 17:17 says, "A friend loves at all times . . ." That pretty much sums it up. When you love

....

with the qualities shown in the definition of love given in 1 Corinthians 13:4–7 you have a clearly defined view of what it means to *be* a godly friend. Replace the word *love* in this passage with the phrase *a godly friend* and you will see what it means to be a godly friend. Let's look: "[A godly friend] is patient, [a godly friend] is kind. [A godly friend] does not envy, . . . does not boast, . . . is not proud. [A godly friend] is not rude, . . . is not self-seeking, . . . is not easily angered, . . . keeps no record of wrongs. [A godly friend] does not delight in evil but rejoices with the truth. [A godly friend] always protects, always trusts, always hopes, always perseveres." Those who would *be* godly friends exhibit special qualities and commitments. Let's look at them here.

KINDNESS MATTERS

The most basic quality of a good friend is kindness, which is a hallmark of love. Whether you are ten or one hundred ten, a little kindness goes a long way toward helping a hurting friend. Ten-year-old Robert* didn't have many friends left. While no one knew much about his family, Robert made up extraordinary stories of a fanciful life that even the kids knew was too good to be true. Most of the boys had stopped playing with him. One mother on the block noticed the tides of childhood cliques turning against Robert and encouraged her son, Anthony, to remain his friend. Anthony invited Robert to KidsFest, his family's church's outreach to children. Robert accepted the invitation and enjoyed KidsFest thoroughly. He learned camping skills and built a birdhouse, which he proudly hung in the tree in his front yard. And he felt loved and welcomed by the kids and adults at church. He went home and told his mom how nicely everyone had treated him.

Robert never talked about his home life when he went to Anthony's house, but he seemed to enjoy spending time there. The family had no idea what a big difference the little bit of kindness they showed him would make.

*The names in this story have been changed.

Some weeks passed, and Robert visited often. One day Anthony's father was out in the yard gardening when he was approached by a tall girl. The "girl" was Robert's brother Joe, dressed as a transvestite, who was struggling with great confusion. He had heard about how kind and accepting Anthony and his family and his church had been. So, when Joe didn't know where to turn, he opened up to the family down the street who professed to be Christians and had demonstrated their beliefs by being nice to his little brother.

Joe needed someone to help him figure some things out. Anthony's mom and dad invited him in for lemonade, listened as he poured out his heart, and didn't know what to say. But they asked if they could pray with him and he agreed. They offered him a Bible, which he accepted and tucked into his purse before he went home.

A few weeks later Anthony's parents found a note taped to their front door. It said, "You have been so kind to my boys. Thank you. If you want to understand more about why Joe struggles as he does, watch 'America's Most Wanted' this Saturday. Signed, Beatrice (Robert and Joe's mother)." The family watched the show and saw a heartbreaking story that had been taking place on their own block without their knowledge. Beatrice and Joe were interviewed in shadows to help conceal their identities and cover their shame.

Joe had been molested by his uncle from earliest childhood without his mother's knowledge. The uncle had also made the boy available for his homosexual friends to use. When Joe's mom discovered the awful truth, she brought charges against her brother. He fled with the help of their mother and stepfather. Beatrice's brother, mother, and stepfather were "America's Most Wanted." Her mother was apprehended and shown in handcuffs. Even though Beatrice had only done what was right and necessary to hold her brother accountable and protect her son, her family turned against her, shunning her and her sons.

The shame and trauma of these events caused Beatrice, Robert, and Joe to isolate themselves. They dared not tell anyone their story for fear of further rejection. Then Anthony was nice to Robert. And Joe ventured down the street to talk. When he, too, was met with kindness, Beatrice was emboldened to tape the first note to their door and run away before she could be seen. The family responded with a note telling Beatrice that they had watched the program and would be praying for her and her sons. Over the next few weeks an overwhelming tale was revealed, bit by bit, in notes Beatrice taped to her neighbors' door before she hurried back inside to hide behind her closed drapes. Finally one of the notes included her phone number. Anthony's mom called. Beatrice wanted to say how much she appreciated the kindness shown her family.

It took time, but one day Beatrice called to ask if she could come down to talk. Anthony's parents made some tea. As Beatrice poured out her heart, they made a list of all the problems that had mounted up in her life. Then they broke the list down into the most basic components: needs for healing, financial support, practical help, spiritual help, new clothes so Beatrice could get a job, courage, and a list of specific things the family needed. Anthony's parents didn't have the resources to help with many of the needs directly, but his father offered to get on the phone to see if he could stir up some help and generosity within the Christian community. No one church could do all that this family needed, but five churches—all of different denominations—offered various kinds of help.

When Women of Faith had a conference nearby, Anthony's mother invited Beatrice to come along with her and several other women who were hurting in various ways. Beatrice felt safe enough to go along. She got dressed up and enjoyed talking and even laughing with the other women. When Point of Grace sang the song about a circle of friends, she looked at her neighbor and mouthed the words, "Thank You!" Over and over Beatrice tried to express how much her neighbors' kindness meant to her. After the conference, the neighbors found another note taped to their door.

In part it read, "I've been in so much mourning. Really, you and those who are befriending me are saving my life. What happened these past two years made me not want to live. I remember when I was praying to get out of the burdens I was in, I really thought it was impossible. . . . No words can describe my gratitude. If I ever come up and survive this it will be because of the kindness I've been shown. I never lost my faith in God, but I was starting to feel that maybe I was unworthy. Thanks so much. I am so overwhelmed. My emotions now are so fragile. Without the love that has been shown me, I don't know where I would be. Forever grateful, Beatrice."

Isn't is staggering to see the effect a little kindness can have? It all began with an eight-year-old boy being nice to another little boy when the other kids on the block turned away. All this family did was show respect for hurting people who were being rejected by others. All they did was tell other Christians about the plight of this single mother and her two boys and ask them to do whatever they could to help. People responded with good deeds, but it was the kindness and respect that helped open the door so the needs could be met. Kindness is amazingly powerful even in small doses, especially when given to those who haven't had much lately. The pop singer Jewel summed it up nicely in a line from a song, "In the end, only kindness matters."

DEVOTION

When people are going through pain, they need a few friends who will personify love in their lives. This love is not predicated on whether their actions or demeanors deserve to be treated with love. It is predicated on the love of the friends and their willingness to be a living embodiment of the love of God. It has been said that people need love the most when they deserve it least. If you are to be a godly friend, you will need to love others out of pure devotion to God and a willingness to love for the sake of love and for the sake of your friends.

There will be times while a friend is suffering and confused, when he or she may not be easy to love. Suffering brings out the worst in people. In fact, the Bible implies that this is part of the process. Suffering purifies us by bringing up the dross within our souls. When the heat is on, people melt like fine gold and all that is impure comes to the surface. That means you may see your friend at his or her worst. That is not when you are to withdraw your love, but rather when you are to love out of devotion to the Lord.

All that we do for others is to be done "as unto the Lord." If you see loving your friend as a demonstration of your love for Jesus (which is how we are told to demonstrate that love; see 1 John 3:16–18, 4:11–12, 19–21), you can express love even when your friend may be acting unlovable.

Consider this example: Mother Teresa of Calcutta loved people whom others saw as unlovable. She explained how she was able to abound in such love—day in and day out—regardless of how unlovely the person on whom she lavished her love. When she became a nun she chose to demonstrate her love for Jesus by loving every person she met as if that person were Jesus. When she loved them, she was loving him.

This understanding came from a story Jesus told about how God will judge our lives. In Jesus' story, the king rewarded those who cared for the unlovely, saying, "I tell you the truth, whatever you did for one of the least of these brothers of mine, you did for me" (Matthew 25:40). But to those who failed to care for "the least of these," the king said, "I tell you the truth, whatever you did not do for one of the least of these, you did not do for me" (Matthew 25:45).

Therefore, all the service Mother Teresa did to "the least of these" she did "as unto the Lord." She demonstrated her love for Jesus in caring for the practical, spiritual, and emotional needs of those who were within her reach. So, too, you can love your friend out of devotion to the Lord Jesus whom you serve.

PURE MOTIVES

People help others for many reasons: Sometimes they offer their love and service purely; other times they have a hidden desire to get something back in the way of applause or looking good in the eyes of others. This story may help you keep your motives in mind.

This is not a story from the Bible, neither is there a historical record that it ever happened. It is given by way of metaphor only. The story goes that Jesus was walking up a mountain with Peter and John. He asked each of them to carry a stone to the top of a steep hill. John picked up a sizable stone and Peter picked up a pebble. When they reached the top of the hill, they were tired and hungry. Jesus took the stone each one carried and turned it into bread. Therefore, John had a sufficient lunch and Peter barely had a morsel. After they ate and rested, Jesus asked them each to carry a stone for him to the bottom of the hill. John again picked up a sizable stone, but Peter hoisted up a huge stone that he was barely able to carry. They walked down the hill. When they arrived at the bottom, Jesus asked Peter to give him the stone. Peter did so, expecting finally to get a good meal, but Jesus tossed the heavy stone into the lake. He did the same with John's stone. Peter was upset. Then Jesus looked at him and said, "I asked you to carry the stone down for me. For whom were you carrying the stone?"

I offer this fictional story because it brings out something you must consider when you are loving a friend through troubled times. For whom are you loving your friend?

We often expect friendship to be reciprocal, and over the long haul it should be. However, when a friend is going through deep waters, he or she may have nothing to give you to nourish your soul. During this season you cannot expect an immediate payoff to what you are giving and doing. This is a time when you need to carry this stone simply for the love of Jesus.

HUMILITY

One of the great temptations you will face while your friend is going through problems is to see yourself as better. Even when Job, who was about as righteous as they come, suffered, his friends were hard-pressed not to see themselves as holier than he was. This is especially true if your friend is suffering in part or whole because of something wrong, risky, or stupid that he or she did. Woodrow Wilson is credited as saying, "You

cannot be friends upon any other terms than upon the terms of equality."
I agree. You must be willing to see your friend as an equal—perhaps one
who has weaknesses you do not have or one who has made wrong
choices you have not made, but as a human being just like you.

Galatians 6:1–2 tells us "Brothers, if someone is caught in a sin, you who
are spiritual should restore him gently. But watch yourself, or you also may
be tempted. Carry each other's burdens, and in this way you will fulfill the
law of Christ." Even when someone is caught in a sin, we are reminded
that we should watch ourselves because—but for the grace of God—we
could be tempted likewise. Don't look down on your friend. It may make
you feel more self-righteous temporarily, but the time will come when you
will go through times of difficulty and you will realize that you are both
made of the same clay. Better to believe God's Word about our shared
human frailty so that you can love your friend as an equal; he or she probably needs the added boost that your loving respect can give.

PROTECTIVE AND RESPECTFUL

When people are going through tough times, others talk. They say all
manner of things that do not build up, but instead tear down those who
are suffering. This is one of the ways to determine who true friends are.
Therefore, to be a godly friend you must make and maintain a firm commitment not to participate in any gossip, slander, innuendo, or backbiting that you may be exposed to with regard to your friends.

Proverbs 16:28 says, "A perverse man stirs up dissension, and a gossip
separates close friends." You must diligently guard yourself not only
from passing on gossip but also from listening to it. The Bible teaches
that we are to get rid of slander of every kind and be kind and compassionate to each other. This is especially important to follow when a friend
becomes the subject of slander and unkind words spoken by others.

Let's look at what Scripture says undermines our relationships with
each other and define specifics so you can make sure you are not hurting
your friend in any of these ways.

- *Gossip:* To gossip is to speak about something or someone when you (and the person to whom you are speaking) are not part of the problem or part of the solution. Scripture says that a talebearer reveals secrets. If a friend confides in you, keep those secrets. Another word associated with gossip is "whisperer." If you feel the need to whisper, you're probably saying something you shouldn't. Commit yourself to not gossip about friends or not tolerate gossip by others. If you are in a conversation that turns to gossip, you might suggest that the people speak more about the matter to God in prayer than they do to each other. That has a way of bringing the subject to a close rather quickly.

- *Backbiting:* Backbiting means to speak against, speak evil, or talk negatively about others behind their backs. If you are doing this, you are not being a godly friend.

- *Slander:* Slander has the most interesting definition when you look at the original biblical language. The word for slander is *diabolos,* from which we derive our word for the devil, specifically when the devil is called the accuser of the brethren. One of Satan's characteristics is to accuse the children of God. That is what started Job's ordeal of suffering. So to slander is to bring accusation against another or to talk like the accuser—the devil. It includes spreading criticism, negative opinion, and innuendo. It involves faultfinding within the church—even if the faults may be real. First Corinthians 13: 6–7 says, "Love does not delight in evil but rejoices with the truth. It always protects. . . ." We all have faults, but part of the way you demonstrate love as a godly friend is to not point out faults or make accusations about a friend to others. Another aspect of slander is to generate or pass along criticism without verifying the facts. (Even Jesus said that by the mouth of two or three witnesses every fact must be established.) So make sure that you do not participate in slander—regardless of whether what is being said has some basis in truth. If you see a problem area or sin in a friend's life, don't talk about it with others. Pray about it, and when appropriate, bring it up with him or her.

- *Double-tongued:* To be double-tongued is to say something to one person and give a different version of it to another. In the New American Standard Version of the Bible, 1 Timothy 3:8 mentions that a church leader should "not be double-tongued" or given to double-talk. The New International Version translates the same phrase as being sincere. These two versions show both the positive and negative sides of the same quality. Being given to double-talk it is the opposite of being sincere. In common vernacular we would call it being two-faced.

Be aware that any of these kinds of communication can destroy your friends' trust in your love. Ask God to help you be a godly friend by filling you with his love. If you fall short in some of these areas, which will happen because of human nature, confess your shortcomings and recommit yourself to being a godly friend and behaving like one.

EMPATHETIC

Empathy is an important quality in those who would be good friends. When Todd was in fourth grade, he was invited to participate in an Excelerated Learning Program for mentally gifted students. A bus picked him up at his home school and transported him to another school in the district where he joined other especially bright youngsters for special classes. At the end of the school day, he was bussed back to his neighborhood school to be picked up by his parents.

While Todd enjoyed the program very much, he was paying a high price socially. Some of the kids from his home school felt envious that he had been singled out as being smarter, so Todd was shunned or teased by the kids who had been his friends in earlier grades. At the other school, where he attended ELP classes, he was the only fourth-grade boy in his group. He didn't have a real friend. Todd felt so miserable he considered dropping out of the program.

His mother and father encouraged him to stick it out through the semester. One day Todd reported that the mother of one of the other kids in the ELP classes had come to speak to their class. Her son had a facial deformity. She explained to the class how he was born with mal-formed facial features, and how doctors had reconstructed his face as best they could. She explained how terribly some of the kids teased him and how hard that was for him. Then she told the class that her son really needed a friend.

Todd's mother pointed out that Todd was probably as much in need of a friend as this other boy. She suggested that they could befriend each other. That sounded like a good idea to Todd. Because Todd had suffered rejection and teasing for the past several months, he could imagine what it must have been like for the other boy to endure that his entire life. His mother didn't have to tell Todd how to approach this boy. Todd had empathy. He simply treated the boy as he wished someone would treat him. The two boys became fast friends for several years and helped each other through a tough time. We can learn from their example.

You already know what it would take for you to be a good friend. Just treat others the way you wish others would treat you. Let your own empathy show you what to do, then do it. Being a good friend is the Golden Rule applied at a fourth-grade level.

....

CHAPTER SEVEN

Boundaries:
Defining Your Commitment and Obligations as a Friend

*B*eing needed by a friend in desperate straits can give you a heady feeling. However, don't let that sensation puff you up so that you commit yourself in ways that are beyond your realistic ability. If you do, your overcommitment will eventually bring disappointment to your friend, and become a burden to you and your family. Besides, it won't do your friend good in the long run. Setting healthy boundaries for your friendship and what you can realistically do to help your friend is very important.

The apostle Paul wrote,

For by the grace given me I say to every one of you: *Do not think of yourself more highly than you ought,* but rather think of yourself with sober judgment, in accordance with the measure of faith God has given you. Just as each of us has one body with many members, and these members do not all have the same function, so *in Christ we who are many form one body, and each member belongs to all the others.* We have different gifts, according to the grace given us. (Romans 12:3–6 , emphasis mine)

....

Here, the Bible shows us that each person is to work with others in the body of Christ. To think that you are the primary helper for someone in need is probably to think more highly of yourself than you ought.

Remember, you play a part—perhaps a vital part, but only a part—in God's overall plan to help your friend. You are not going to be your friend's savior—no matter how spiritual you are. While this can be a let-down, it can also be a relief. But however it strikes you, it is essential that you agree with this biblical truth in heart and action. Setting and enforcing healthy relational boundaries with your friend demonstrates your recognition that you are only part of the overall help God will provide. This chapter will show you why this is important to set limits, where to draw the lines, how to communicate your boundaries to your hurting friend, how to reset improper boundaries, and how to practice enforcing healthy relational boundaries.

Michelle is a high-energy helper. Along with her husband, she is a trusted lay-minister in her church. Together they provide a ministry of marriage reconciliation for estranged couples. In temperament, she's the kind of woman whose intelligence, zeal, vision, and compassion cause her to seek to do great things in God's kingdom. These attributes also cause others to naturally gravitate to her when they need help. She has survived troubled waters in her marriage, so she comes across as one who cares, who's been there, and who knows God well enough to make a real difference in the lives of others. All of this is true and good as long as Michelle maintains healthy boundaries.

This great combination of attributes also has a downside. If Michelle is not careful, people come to expect more of her than she can realisti-cally give. A story she has shared illustrates the dangers of failing to set relational boundaries when your friend is going through hell.

When Michelle and her husband first began their ministry to estranged couples seeking reconciliation, she took a hands-on approach with almost every woman who turned to her for help. Her friendly manner made people think of her as one of their best friends, when—in reality—they were acquaintances she was ministering to. One woman who relied heavily on Michelle called her regularly while her marriage was in crisis. Michelle enjoyed feeling needed and admired as someone who could help. So she took the calls, sometimes even when they interfered with her responsibilities at home as a wife and mother.

This was not a big problem at first, but the more she welcomed the calls, the more often they seemed to come. At first, the woman called only when she had a major crisis. After a while, she increased the frequency of her calls, calling to report relatively minor incidents in her troubled relationship with her husband. Michelle sensed that she should correct this, but she didn't want to hurt the woman's feelings. Meanwhile, her family's resentment grew whenever Michelle was on the phone with this woman instead of focusing on them.

Michelle and her family took a much needed vacation. She and her husband were nearing burn-out, but some time away refreshed them. They decided to come home a day early to try to get their house in order before they had to dive back into their hectic daily routines. Michelle wasn't even going to answer the phone, but when it rang she grabbed it out of instinct.

It was the woman who had become dependent on her. She said that she *had* to talk, that Michelle was her only friend, and that she was desperate because she'd had to deal with the relational upheavals alone while Michelle was unavailable. (Michelle detected more than a hint of resentment over her lack of availability.) Michelle looked around her at the piles of laundry from their vacation, the packed suitcases still stacked by the door, the expressions on the faces of her husband and children— and she realized that she had to draw the line.

She calmly said, "I am very sorry, but I cannot help you now. My family is still on vacation and I choose to be with them."

"But you're my only friend," came the reply.

Michelle tried to add perspective: "We're not even due back until tomorrow. I wasn't supposed to answer the phone. We haven't even unpacked. I'm sorry. I will be back at the church day after tomorrow. I can talk then, but I cannot help you now."

The woman hung up on her.

This was a wake-up call. In recounting this story for a class on how to help someone in crisis, Michelle demonstrates the dangers of promising more than you can deliver. She warns against operating without healthy boundaries. In retrospect, Michelle has come to realize that her lack of boundaries all along contributed to this woman's pain at a time when she was already suffering. She shares the story to highlight why, when you are helping a hurting person, you must set healthy boundaries.

WHY WE NEED TO SET HEALTHY BOUNDARIES

The following reasons to set healthy boundaries can all be seen in Michelle's story. See if these ring any warning bells about any of your relationships.

- If you don't set realistic boundaries up front, your friends may have unrealistic expectations of you. These lead to disappointment when you cannot do what your friends expect.
- Without healthy boundaries, your friends' needs can intrude on your family obligations. This leads to resentment and problems you'll have to deal with when family members' rightful priority in your life becomes usurped.
- There will be increased stress in all areas of your life. The more time and emotional energy you give to friends, the less you will have to give at work and home. Those to whom you have made primary commitments will tug at you. There will be added emotional stress if family conflicts arise and feelings get hurt because it appears that you care more for others' needs than for your family's.
- Your friends' reliance on you as a primary helper may keep them from seeking the full spectrum of help they need.
- Your lack of boundaries sets up unrealistic expectations. When friends act on those expectations, the time will come when reality

finally crashes down. People will be hurt. Your feelings may be hurt because others seem ungrateful in demanding more than you can give, especially after you have given so much. Friends may feel hurt because you set up the unrealistic expectations, then seemingly broke your promise when you finally had to draw the line. There may be added embarrassment to friends who act on what you had implied. These hurt feelings only add to your friends' burdens—and to yours.

- When you set up boundaries belatedly, others may interpret this as rejection or a lack of love.
- Friends who are suffering have raging emotions and what sometimes feels like an ocean of ongoing needs. If you hold out the promise of limitless help and solace, your needy friends will naturally be drawn to your openness like an ocean is drawn into a bay. You do not truly help anyone by representing yourself as completely open. The promise of unlimited help is not humanly possible to keep, but to a person in need, it is almost irresistible. If you set up no boundaries, you may find yourself drowning in a friend's overwhelming needs until you cry out for help.
- If you do not have healthy boundaries while friends are going through difficulty, you will eventually get burned out. The symptoms include growing resentment, alternating feelings of guilt for what you are not doing and self-justification for what have done and cannot continue to do, feeling too tired, avoiding your friend, shutting down emotionally, and a growing need to escape. The result will be impaired health and relationships.
- If you don't have set boundaries in terms of what is appropriate to share, you may find yourself hearing things you don't want to know and feeling uncomfortable with the level of disclosure.
- Without healthy relational boundaries, people end up trespassing against each other without realizing it.

Setting your boundaries is a matter of defining where others' lives end and yours begins. All these reasons for setting healthy boundaries are given to encourage you to consider defining and communicating your boundaries as doing your friends a favor. When you do, you protect against trespasses that lead to real problems. If you set healthy boundaries today, you relieve others of having to forgive you in the future for something you can prevent. You will spare your friends hurt, fend off offenses before they occur, and prevent conflicts.

CONSIDER WHY SETTING HEALTHY BOUNDARIES MAY BE HARD FOR YOU

One thing you may need to think about is whether your lack of boundaries indicates an area of need in *your* life. Some people compensate for shortages in their own lives by being needed by others. They distract themselves from their own issues by finding someone whose problems are worse and focusing their attention away from themselves. It is usually good to help others. However, if helping others is a way of avoiding primary responsibilities or problems that require attention in your own life, this kind of distraction is not good.

This kind of behavior has been called codependency in recent years. But whatever you call it, a preoccupation with helping others to the detriment of yourself and/or your primary relationships is not in keeping with God's best for you. Therefore, if you find it difficult to set healthy boundaries, if you seem to lose your purpose in life when you are not desperately needed, if your God-given priorities are out of order, you should look at this more closely. You may need the guidance of a counselor or pastor to be able to see clearly. But if this chapter is especially hard for you, talk to someone you trust about these issues.

WHERE TO DRAW BOUNDARY LINES

Once you're convinced that having healthy boundaries is necessary, you have to decide where to draw those lines. I believe the overall design of our lives is given in God's Word. What I will do here is focus on that design and suggest how you can use biblical principles to lay the groundwork for your specific boundaries.

God gives us each personal responsibility for our lives. Galatians 6:2 says, "Carry each other's burdens, and in this way you will fulfill the law of Christ." Galatians 6:4–5 adds, "Each one should test his own actions. Then he can take pride in himself, without comparing himself to somebody else, for each one should carry his own load." Here we see the balance of helping others carry a load that is impossible for any person to carry alone and the need for personal responsibility for carrying our own responsibilities.

The balance to this is the idea conveyed in verse four, where each one is to carry his or her own "load." The Greek word used there can be translated "knapsack." We are all responsible for carrying our basic responsibilities, which include:

- Having a personal relationship with God
- Fulfilling responsibilities in primary family relationships
- Making moral choices and bearing the consequences for those choices
- Taking responsibility for our own soul: mind, will, and emotions
- Doing good works (which, according to Ephesians 2:10, God has prepared for us in advance)
- Keeping personal commitments
- Struggling with personal sin (including addictions) and recovering from the ravages of sin

ALLOW YOUR FRIENDS TO CARRY THEIR OWN RESPONSIBILITIES

One key place to start in drawing healthy boundaries with friends is to make sure that you are not trying to do for them the things God considers part of their "knapsacks" of personal responsibility. You cannot control whether a friend chooses to sin. You dare not intrude in a friend's primary family relationships with spouse, children, or parents. You are not responsible for shielding someone from the natural consequences of his or her actions. These are areas where the best you can do is to advise and encourage friends to make sure they are living in keeping with God's commands and guidance in the Bible.

EXAMINE YOUR PRIMARY RELATIONAL COMMITMENTS

You must also start to define your limits by making sure you are being faithful to your primary responsibilities. For example, if you are married, you do not neglect your mate because a friend's crisis takes precedence for you. It should not. If you have children, you are accountable before God to care for their needs. Therefore, to repeatedly neglect the valid needs of your children because your friend is in trouble is out of line. If you have committed yourself to an employer as an employee, you are to fulfill your obligation to work heartily, as if you were doing it for the Lord himself. It is not right to excuse poor performance on the job because you are trying to help a friend in trouble. You have primary commitments that must be respected.

This is not to say that you cannot make arrangements with those to whom you are responsible in order to help a friend in times of dire need. You can make arrangements with your mate to take some extra time to care for your friend. However, if your mate does not agree, you need to trust God to find your friend help elsewhere. If you have children, you can delegate some of their care to other responsible persons to allow you to help your friend. Or you may be able to incorporate your mate and children into a project to help your friend. This is a great way to live out your faith before your kids. If you need to take time away from work temporarily, don't just take the time without asking. Make arrangements that are fair to your employer. These God-given commitments and responsibilities will provide clear-cut boundaries to the person who is willing to accept such limitations.

LOOK AT THE DEPTH AND CLOSENESS
OF THE RELATIONSHIP

Another determining factor regarding how much you are to involve yourself in a friend's life during a time of trouble would be the depth and closeness of the relationship. Even Jesus did not call everyone his friend. You have many acquaintances, some casual friends, some longtime friends, and some who are in your inner circle of close devoted friends. It is appropriate to determine your level of involvement with someone based on the previous depth and closeness of the relationship. Proverbs 18:24 acknowledges this when it says, "A man of many companions may come to ruin, but there is a friend who sticks closer than a brother." If your friend in need is one who sticks closer than a brother, you will rightfully involve yourself more deeply than you would if a casual acquaintance from work were going through something. You may call each your friend, but there are relevant distinctions that will help you decide how much you can give.

Michelle made the mistake of allowing a woman who was really only an acquaintance to believe that she was a close friend. To the woman, Michelle was probably one of her closest friends at the time, but that was not truly the way Michelle saw her. The result was that the woman was hurt and offended when she realized that she considered Michelle more of a friend than Michelle considered her. It's better to recognize the true level of relationship and communicate that level of concern than to feign more.

DETERMINE HOW MUCH TIME AND ENERGY
YOU CAN REALISTICALLY OFFER

Another way to set boundaries is to look realistically at your time and energy commitments. You really can only do so much! You may wish that you could stay at a friend's side while she waits for her husband to come out of his coma. Or you may want to take meals to another friend and his family every night until his wife recovers from surgery. But what you wish you could do and what you actually have time and energy to do may differ greatly. Don't let your good intentions lead the way when you are offering help. Start there, but then fit what you wish you could do into the limiting framework of what you actually have time and energy to do. That will help you shape realistic boundaries.

CHECK THE MORAL BOUNDARY LINES

There are also moral boundary lines that you may need to draw, depending on your friend's situation and what has been asked of you. Determine that you will not participate in anything "to help" your friend that would require you to violate God's commands, for example, lying or making up a false alibi to "help" someone out. Other moral boundaries you might set could include committing to not share anything your friend tells you in confidence, not agreeing to participate in anything sinful or cover up sinful behavior, and promising never to gossip or slander your friend or the people who may be in opposition to your friend. You can take a careful look at the situation and find Bible principles that come into play. Then decide how these can help you clarify the kind of behavior you will and will not participate in yourself. Make it clear that your love and help cannot go beyond your moral boundaries. This is not a reflection of a lack of love for your friend, but rather it shows your overriding commitment to live as God would have you live—even if your friend takes it as a lack of love.

THE BOUNDARY LINE OF FREE WILL

It is right to set your own boundaries according to God's Word, but you don't have the right to try to force others to do what you believe is correct—even if it is the way God clearly spells it out in the Bible. If you do, you are overstepping your friends' God-given free will.

God himself will not violate the boundary of free will. Each person stands before God as an individual. He doesn't make us into his puppets.

He allows each of us to choose how we will live. God gives us clear moral standards of right and wrong. He warns us of the consequences if we disobey and tells of the blessings if we obey. He explains that we will not be able to live in obedience by our own power and offers to fill us with his Spirit so we are empowered to fulfill his law. God makes all of this clear, but he never oversteps the boundary of our free will. Neither should you with your friends. You can do for others what God does for us, but you cannot make your friends comply. God has not failed to love and guide us when we choose to disobey, and you have not failed to love your friends if you point out the right moral road and they choose not to take it. For example if you have a friend who is filled with hatred toward someone and refuses to forgive that person, you can gently point out how this errs from what the Bible commands. But you should draw the line before you assume a friend is in sin when that is not clearly the case. You should also beware of pointing out the sin in your friend's life if your own sinful patterns have yet to be corrected. Jesus warned against pointing out the speck of dust in a friend's eye when there is a log in your own.

EXAMINE THE BOUNDARIES
OF YOUR ABILITIES AND LIMITATIONS

Remember that you are part of a body. Each part has its own design in keeping with its purpose. Each part also has its own limitations. So, too, you have certain abilities and limitations. These may be spiritual gifts, such as a gift of mercy or giving. These may be natural abilities, such as being able to withstand the sight of blood in an emergency. Whatever your particular makeup and the situations you find yourself in with your friend, there will be some things you are designed to handle and some things you simply can't stomach. That's OK. Be honest with yourself about what you can and cannot give. A person who lacks the gift of mercy but has a gift for giving might better serve a friend in trouble by providing financial help than to try to visit the hospital every day. We should all do our best to be kind, but the person who is gifted in mercy should be the one sitting by the bedside. If you find yourself unable to do something, accept that limitation. Do what you can. Allow your recognition of your personal abilities, giftings, and limitations to help shape the kind of commitment you can make.

THE BEAUTY OF WORKING TOGETHER
TO HELP SOMEONE IN NEED

There is a beautiful side to recognizing our limitations and setting realistic boundaries when we set out to help a friend in trouble. We get a chance to see the body of Christ function as it was intended to. When this happens, people see God at work, he gets the glory, and no one gets exhausted.

I was speaking at a women's retreat when we received word that a family in the church had suffered yet another tragedy. This family had been through tough times: They had lost their home; the wife had become pregnant and given up her job; they were without insurance, then the husband's employer went out of business. So the congregation had been praying for them. The wife had given birth a few days before, and while we were at the retreat, the husband was in an accident that broke both of his legs. This family was in dire need of help, and many of its friends were gathered together at the retreat.

Since we were talking about using our gifts and abilities for God's purposes, we decided to work together to help this family. First, I asked for someone who has a recognized ability to organize. Everyone in the room pointed to one woman. She was appointed as the organizer or the brains of the body. Then I asked for those who have a way with words and want to be used by God in writing. The five or so who raised their hands were appointed to write notes of encouragement to the family every day. I asked who actually liked cleaning house. Several women raised their hands. I asked if each could spare two hours each week to provide household help for the family. Then we asked for those who are great cooks and like making meals. Hands shot up. I asked who sensed a calling as intercessors or prayer warriors. They agreed to cover the family in prayer. Those with the gift of giving set out to accumulate funds to help the family get back on their feet financially. We continued thinking of what this family could possibly need and asked for someone who felt particularly able or gifted in each area. All these people reported to the woman who agreed to organize them. She planned out a weekly calendar so that no one person gave more than a small and enjoyable contribution (enjoyable because it was what they liked to do and were realistically able to do). We didn't tell the family what was coming.

In the months that followed I heard reports that this group of Christian women worked together as the body of Christ beautifully. No one thought of herself more highly than she ought to think, and yet they all were able to praise God at the tremendous level of love and help they were able to give their friend and her family in this time of crisis. This could only work because the boundaries were clearly drawn and no one person was left to do too much. You can't do it all, but you can contribute to a cooperative effort where everything can get done to the glory of God.

COMMUNICATE YOUR BOUNDARIES

The best way to communicate your boundaries is simply, honestly, and with love. You need to include four items of information: (1) an expression of how much you care, (2) what help you can offer during this time of need, (3) your limitations, which includes where you draw the lines, and (4) why you have these particular limits.

You might say something like this, (1) "I am so sorry to hear about what is happening. I can't even imagine how you must be feeling, but I am sorry you are hurting. (2) I would be willing to take the children during the daytime or bring over meals if that would help. Or if you need to talk you can call me after I put my kids to bed at nine. (3) I'm sorry I can't talk before then but (4) our family is so busy from the time the kids get home from school until bedtime that I wouldn't be able to be much comfort to you."

Don't say clichéd phrases that offer more than you can realistically do. For example, comments like, "If you ever need anything just call," or "Call me anytime," set up unrealistic expectations unless you are prepared to actually be available anytime to do anything. Most people can't make such commitments and keep them.

If you have previously set up a relationship with insufficient boundaries or allowed someone to encroach into your life to the point where that person is taking precedence over your primary relationships (family) and responsibilities (at home and work) you can correct the situation. This must be done carefully since your friend may really have come to depend on you. And this must be done with sensitivity because a person who is going through difficulty is already stressed, emotionally spent, and may not be thinking clearly. You must also be willing to assess your part in setting up the relationship as it is. The more you can accept responsibility for giving out signals that contributed to the lack of boundaries, the easier it will be for your friend to adjust to a new relationship with healthy boundaries.

Let's use the case of Michelle Williams and the woman who looked to her for help. Michelle let the relationship go without healthy boundaries until a crisis point occurred. As a result, the woman's feelings were hurt; she hung up the phone and broke off the relationship. Here I will suggest how such a breach—which severed the opportunity for Michelle to extend help and care to this woman—could be avoided.

Start by assessing specifically where you are feeling uncomfortable with the relationship and where you or your family senses your friend is overstepping into your lives. Is it the amount of time and attention required? Is it the time of day or night when your friend is calling for your involvement? Is it the emotional demands? Is it the level of relationship presumed? Once you have a clear definition of what is over the line (that line you didn't recognize or announce earlier in the relationship), define where your actual limits need to be drawn. Michelle would have noted that she felt uncomfortable with the woman breaking into Michelle's family time, assuming that her extremity should take precedence over Michelle's responsibilities at home, and intruding into Michelle's vacation.

Take stock of what you have implied or stated that gave your friend reason to believe that the current level of involvement and relationship was OK with you. The more you can take responsibility for inviting your friend into your life, the less awkwardness and defensiveness your friend will feel. Be generous but honest in taking responsibility for where you allowed the relationship to go. Michelle would have noted that she implied by her helpful, friendly, and caring manner that she was this woman's personal friend rather than an acquaintance with whom she was friendly; and that she gave the impression that the woman could call any time she was experiencing a problem in her marriage.

Decide on what boundaries you need to set, using the guidelines given earlier in this chapter. Then set a time to talk with your friend. When you meet do the following: (1) State your love and care for your friend. (2) Admit that what you wish you could do to help exceeds what you can realistically carry out. (3) Apologize for giving the impression that you were available more than you actually are. If you have given specific promises of help or availability that you cannot continue to honor, state these followed by something like, "I really wish I could be there for you in these ways, but I overestimated myself. I really can't accept three or four calls a day." (4) Then follow the guidelines for setting healthy boundaries.

You will need to allow your friend to process the feelings that arise. You will also need to reaffirm your love and concern. After you have clarified what you actually can offer in terms of support, help, and availability, repeat that the change in boundaries is not a personal rejection. Rather it is a way to preserve the relationship long-term. One other thing you may do to help your friend make this transition is to plan ahead to suggest others who can take up the slack in areas where you are drawing back.

Michelle could have done this for her friend by saying, "I really do care about you and your marital problems. I know I came across as someone you could confide in at any time, but I did not take into account the needs of my family. I realize now that I offered more than I can actually supply, and that has had ramifications for me at home. I am sorry for having to pull back from previous commitments I made outright and implied by my manner. But from now on I will only be able to take your calls at the church office. I know that your problems won't stop just because I go home, so I spoke with a few others who work with our ministry, and they said you could call them after hours if you need to, but you'll need to check with them to see how late you can call. I hope you don't take this personally. It says more about me than it does about you. I just overcommitted myself. I still care about you and your situation. I will still pray for you as the Lord brings you to mind, and I hope you will call when I am in the office. That way, I can give you the full attention you need. I really do still care. I hope you understand."

If you have a problem setting healthy boundaries, get someone to help you. Your family is a good place to start, especially if your lack of boundaries with your friend has stepped over into their rightful claim on your time and attention. They can help you find the right boundaries. If you feel guilty about setting boundaries or fear that your friend could not survive without your unlimited involvement, I suggest you speak with a pastor or counselor. This may constitute what Romans 12:3–6 refers to as thinking of yourself more highly than you ought. You may need help to understand why *you* need to be needed so much that it interferes with the healthy, balanced, and well-prioritized life God intends for you.

Overall, remind yourself that setting healthy boundaries in relationship will have good long-term effects. You will not experience the negative effects of a relationship where you or your family are feeling trespassed against. Your friend will not develop an improper dependence on one person over a proper dependence on God and a body of people working together to express the love of God. When you set healthy boundaries, you will do your part without being exhausted so that you can continue to be a friend and a source of support over the long haul.

CHAPTER EIGHT
....

Advice on Giving Godly Advice
(Including What Not to Say)

*S*uppose one of your closest friends came home from work fuming about something while you were visiting his house with some other close friends who are used to offering each other advice. Without much prodding, your friend tells the group about this guy around the office who's been showing disrespect for him. Might you toss in your two cents worth about how you wouldn't take that kind of treatment? Might you throw out a few ideas about how your friend could put his coworker in his place? Or would you prayerfully ask God for wisdom and carefully consider your words before offering advice to a distressed friend? Your approach to giving advice to anyone who is caught up in a stressful situation can have life and death consequences. So, be careful!

People going through crisis or difficult times in life turn to their friends for advice. This is as God would have it. Proverbs 27:9–10 says, "Perfume and incense bring joy to the heart, and the pleasantness of one's friend springs from his earnest counsel. Do not forsake your friend and the friend of your father, and do not go to your brother's house when disaster strikes you—better a neighbor nearby than a brother far away."

If you are nearby when a friend is going through hell, God can use you to give earnest—and godly—counsel.

I hope the following list of *dos* and *don'ts* of giving godly advice and counsel will help you help your friend. It is not a comprehensive list, but I have tested these things by Scripture and seen them applied successfully.

- *Don't just give your own opinion.* At a time like this, your friend needs to discover what God would have him or her do to make wise decisions. Beware of casually offering your opinion as though it were equal to God's wisdom. A man named Haman was a high official in the administration of King Xerxes of Persia when Esther was queen. He was outraged because he wasn't getting the respect he thought he deserved. A Jewish man named Mordecai (who was the queen's relative unbeknown to Haman) refused to bow to him. So Haman went home and called together his friends and Zeresh, his wife. The Bible tells us that

Haman boasted to them about his vast wealth, his many sons, and all the ways the king had honored him and how he had elevated him above the other nobles and officials. "And that's not all," Haman added. "I'm the only person Queen Esther invited to accompany the king to the banquet she gave. And she has invited me along with the king tomorrow. But all this gives me no satisfaction as long as I see that Jew Mordecai sitting at the king's gate."

His wife Zeresh and all his friends said to him, "Have a gallows built, seventy-five feet high, and ask the king in the morning to have Mordecai hanged on it. Then go with the king to the dinner and be happy." This suggestion delighted Haman, and he had the gallows built. (Esther 5:11–14)

This sounded like great advice coming from Haman's wife and friends. Their emotions were stirred by their friend's plight and they offered their opinions. However, not one of them sought God's will. Not one of them knew the whole story. Can you imagine how these friends felt the next day when they saw Haman's dead body hanging from the gallows they had urged him to have built? You can read the book of Esther to see how quickly the tables turned for Haman. The point I wish to highlight is how Haman was destroyed because he followed his friends' advice when they were only giving their opinion. There is grave danger in throwing out mere human opinion when your friend is in crisis. Don't do it. Seek God before you offer your advice.

- *Don't offer human wisdom as if it were God's wisdom.* There are characteristic differences between human or earthly wisdom and God's wisdom. Check whether your wisdom has any of the markers of earthly wisdom. If it does, stop yourself before offering advice born of such so-called wisdom. James wrote,

> Who is wise and understanding among you? Let him show it by his good life, by deeds done in the humility that comes from wisdom. But if you harbor bitter envy and selfish ambition in your hearts, do not boast about it or deny the truth. Such "wisdom" does not come down from heaven but is earthly, unspiritual, of the devil. For where you have envy and selfish ambition, there you find disorder and every evil practice. (James 3:13–16)

- *Don't give specific advice when you don't know all the facts.* There are always at least two sides to every story. Beware of telling your friend what you think would be the right thing to do if you have no way of knowing the whole story or situation. Instead guide your friend to biblical principles by which he or she can make decisions. What may seem like a good thing to do, from what you know of the situation, may not be good for all concerned. Nor may it be the right thing, given the parts of the story your friend has failed to mention.
- Don't say, *"This is God's word to you,"* if you are not sure it is. There is sometimes the temptation to add weight to our pronouncements

by declaring, "Thus says the Lord!" Any word given as "a word from the Lord" must stand up to the test of a true prophet. Deuteronomy addresses this question, saying, "If what a prophet proclaims in the name of the Lord does not take place or come true, that is a message the Lord has not spoken. That prophet has spoken presumptuously" (18:22). Beware of speaking presumptuously in the name of the Lord.

There will be times you will feel deeply impressed that the Lord has a specific direction your friend should take. By all means, share your sense of gravity and how you felt the Holy Spirit impressing you of this as you prayed. Just make sure you do not try to manipulate your friend into doing what you think is right by making it sound like a direct word from the Lord unless you truly believe it is.

- *Don't put a spiritual Band-Aid on a deep wound.* You may want your friend to feel better as soon as possible. However, there are times when God allows people to go through seasons of pain, times when God wants them to get help for a specific problem or a deep wound. As a friend of someone who is deeply wounded, your aim should be to help your friend get the appropriate help to deal with the full depth of the wound. If you offer a few nice Bible verses or make assurances that everything will be fine, you may actually interfere with your friend's getting the healing care or correction he or she needs.

God reprimanded the priests in the prophet Jeremiah's time for doing this. Jeremiah 6:14 says, "They dress the wound of my people as though it were not serious. 'Peace, peace,' they say, when there is no peace." The people had turned away from God. They continually deceived one another and lived in idolatry, adultery, and all manner of sin. They were in big trouble with God. Jeremiah was willing to treat their spiritual wounds as seriously as God did. He went on to write, "Since my people are crushed, I am crushed; I mourn, and horror grips me. Is there no balm in Gilead? Is there no physician there? Why then is there no healing for the wound of my people?" (Jeremiah 8:21–22)

Jeremiah knew that those who did not see the seriousness of their condition would not get appropriate help. If your friend is dealing with any kind of serious condition—whether spiritual, emotional, relational, or physical—don't make light of it as if everything is fine. Instead, help your friend take the situation and condition seriously enough to find out what is causing the wound or pain. Urge him or her to find appropriate care to deal with the real condition.

- *Don't apply your limited experience or knowledge to a friend's situation.* One mistake people often make is to try to apply what worked for them in one situation to someone else's life when the situations are not the same. For instance, if you have gone through depression and a friend is depressed, you may explain what you did to get out of depression. You may even get irritated if what worked for you doesn't seem to work for your friend. You may assume that he or she is not really trying to get out of the depression or is wallowing in self-pity when that is not the case at all. The problem here is that depression can spring from various causes. What worked in your situation probably worked because it addressed whatever caused you to feel depressed. Rather than try to apply what worked in your situation to another's situation, try to help your friend find the cause of the depression and deal with it appropriately. Just because you have been through something similar, don't assume that your way out is the only way out for your friend.

- *Don't treat the gray areas not addressed directly by Scripture as if they are black and white.* There are some issues that are clearly dealt with in Scripture. However, there are many situations in which people must be guided by the Holy Spirit and their own consciences. There are some things that can be right for one Christian and wrong for another because one's conscience allows more freedom than the other's. In New Testament times, Christians argued over whether it was right for a Christian to eat meat sacrificed to idols or to drink wine. Paul addressed these gray areas by saying, "So whatever you believe about these things keep between yourself and God. Blessed is the man who does not condemn himself by what he approves. But the man who has doubts is condemned if he eats, because his eating is not from faith; and everything that does not come from faith is sin" (Romans 14:22–23).

Here the Bible allows that there are some areas of conscience where each person must determine what God allows and not condemn others whose consciences allow them to do something else. For example, you may be convicted by the Holy Spirit or convinced by your denomination's stance on alcohol that you should never touch a drop; to do so would violate your conscience. Or you may find that half a glass of wine helps you relax at the end of a hard day and you may not have any pang of conscience against doing so; perhaps your denomination has no restriction against drinking. My point is neither to condone nor condemn having a glass of wine. This is one of many issues left to one's conscience and the Holy Spirit. The Bible condemns drunkenness, but there are also some passages that condone drinking some alcohol.

So do not treat the gray areas as black and white. If you don't have a clear conscience about something because it is not part of your spiritual tradition, or because God has shown you that it is a danger for you, or you lack the faith to do it, for you to do so would be sin. However, you cannot dictate that your friend's conscience be guided by yours in areas that the Bible leaves as a matter of conscience.

- *Don't require a spiritual remedy for everything.* While we are spiritual beings and all aspects of our lives have a spiritual dimension, we are also physical and intellectual beings. God designed body, mind, and spirit to interrelate. To whatever degree your friend is dealing with spiritual issues, a spiritual remedy is called for; to whatever degree the issues are physical, medical, emotional, or relational, the remedy should match the source of the problem. In the Bible, when Timothy was having stomach problems, Paul recommended a medicinal approach rather than prayer alone (see 1 Timothy 5:23). The help your friend needs may not be limited to spiritual help.

- *Don't just explain what to do; help your friend find meaning and understanding.* Sometimes when people ask for answers, what they really wants is someone willing to explore their questions, to help them discover the meaning of their lives. If you are aware of this, there may be times to refrain from answering a friend's questions while joining in his or her quest for understanding.
- *Don't shy away from pointing out sin if it is part of the problem.* The prophet Daniel faced a delicate situation. From his youth, he had spent his life in exile, serving as an advisor to King Nebuchadnezzar of Babylon. Daniel had seen three of his good friends thrown into a fiery furnace as punishment for refusing to worship a ninety-foot-high golden statue of the king, whose life was filled with idolatry and pride. God miraculously delivered the three from their fiery deaths, which gained the king's respect for their God, but surely left Daniel aware of the danger faced by anyone who confronted the king with his own sin.

  Years later King Nebuchadnezzar had a troubling dream that none of his magicians or diviners could interpret, so he called for Daniel. After the king related his dream, Daniel sought God's interpretation on the king's behalf. God revealed that the dream was a warning that judgment was about to fall on Nebuchadnezzar; God intended to deal with the king's pride. Daniel found himself in the awkward position of having to point out the king's sin and the coming judgment from God without becoming the target of the king's fury.

You may find yourself in a similar situation with a friend. If you are afraid to tell that friend the hard truth, you may be glad to know that even Daniel felt fear in his situation. The Bible says, "Then Daniel (also called Belteshazzar) was greatly perplexed for a time, and his thoughts terrified him. So the king said, 'Belteshazzar, do not let the dream or its meaning alarm you'" (Daniel 4:19). So Daniel found the balance between clearly explaining that the dream meant that God was about to judge the king for his sin, and offering wise counsel as to how he might minimize the negative consequences. Daniel told him, "Therefore, O king, be pleased to accept my advice: Renounce your sins by doing what is right, and your wickedness by being kind to the oppressed. It may be that then your prosperity will continue" (Daniel 4:27). The king followed Daniel's advice for a time and the judgment was postponed.

Likewise, if a time comes when you see clearly how your friend needs to repent of sin, and your friend asks you for advice, be sensitive but don't shy away from pointing out sin and showing how it can be overcome. You may be able to avert or at least postpone the negative consequences that will surely come from disobeying God.

- *Don't assume that your friend is somehow to blame for suffering.* We can learn a lot from Job's friends. Throughout the book of Job, God reveals a dialogue between Job and a few of his closest friends. They could not understand how someone who seemed as upright as Job could experience such severe suffering. He lost everything. His ten children were killed in a freak accident. He was stricken with disease. And his wife told him that he should just curse God and die. But Job refused to accept the blame for his own suffering and refused to give up his faith in God.

Job's friends' discourses keep going back to the same theme: They assumed that Job must have done something to deserve what happened to him. They even went so far as to say that his children must have sinned and therefore deserved to be killed. Their accusations were of no help to Job; in fact they became an added source of suffering for him. Unknown to any of them, Job's suffering came because of Satan—also known as the accuser. In the end of the book, God made it known to Job's friends that they were way off base when they said that Job had brought his suffering on himself. Job had to pray for them so they would not be punished for their mistaken approach to his suffering. Don't make the same mistake they made. You may want to read the book of Job to learn what not to say to a hurting friend.

THINGS YOU SHOULD DO
WHEN OFFERING ADVICE TO A HURTING FRIEND

- *Do maintain a humble attitude.* No matter how spiritual or brilliant you may be, any advice you offer while looking down on your friend will not be well received. Consider the humility shown by C. S. Lewis when responding to his friend, Sheldon Vanauken, while he was grieving the death of his wife. Although Lewis was a highly respected educator and author, listen to the humility with which he prefaced his advice to his friend. "Think of me as a fellow-patient in the same hospital who, having been admitted a little earlier, could give some advice."[1]
- *Do listen more than you talk when your friend is hurting.* Job's friends were a great comfort to him for the first week after disaster struck his life.

When Job's three friends, Eliphaz the Temanite, Bildad the Shuhite and Zophar the Naamathite, heard about all the troubles that had come upon him, they set out from their homes and met together by agreement to go and sympathize with him and comfort him. When they saw him from a distance, they could hardly recognize him; they began to weep aloud, and they tore their robes and sprinkled dust on their heads. Then they sat on the ground with him for seven days and seven nights. No one said a word to him, because they saw how great his suffering was. (Job 2:11–13)

Job's three friends did great while they were silent. But they got into trouble once they started trying to diagnose his condition and explain what he should do to find relief. Once they started talking, they ended up being reprimanded by Job and by God. When someone is suffering terribly, you can't go wrong by listening more than you talk. And when you do open your mouth, be careful that what you are saying is true and helpful. When in doubt about whether to say something, be quiet.

- *Do ask for and expect God's wisdom.* The Bible states, "If any of you lacks wisdom, he should ask God, who gives generously to all without finding fault, and it will be given to him. But when he asks, he must believe and not doubt, because he who doubts is like a wave of the sea, blown and tossed by the wind. That man should not think he will receive anything from the Lord; he is a double-minded man, unstable in all he does" (James 1:5–8). When you don't know what to advise your friend, ask God for wisdom and expect him to give it to you.

When you believe you have wise advice to give, check to see whether it is in keeping with the characteristics of godly wisdom given in James 3:17, which says, "But the wisdom that comes from heaven is first of all pure; then peace-loving, considerate, submissive, full of mercy and good fruit, impartial and sincere."

- *Do direct your friend to make decisions on the basis of the Bible.* If your friend asks you what to do in a particular situation, say something like, "I can't say exactly what you should do or how you should handle your situation, but let's look at what the Bible says about it." Then guide your friend to Bible passages that address the situation. Be willing to discuss how to apply the verses. In this way, you may end up helping your friend to decide to do the very thing you could have suggested on the basis of your knowledge of the Bible. However, by going to the Bible directly, you help your friend think through what God has to say and apply God's Word to his or her own life. If your friend is unfamiliar with the Bible, you can use this time to introduce him or her to God's Word as a source of comfort and real help in times of trouble. You may find it helpful to get a book that arranges Bible verses according to need or topic.

- *Do help your friend learn and apply biblical principles.* You will not always be with your friend to help him or her make decisions. Therefore, it will be helpful to share Bible principles that can be used for general decision making. The following section provides some basic Bible principles that will help in many situations.

BIBLICAL PRINCIPLES YOUR FRIEND
CAN LEARN TO APPLY

Many times there are no easy answers! Friends may come to you with situations that are so perplexing or potentially life-changing that you dare not give specific advice. But you can point out the principles that can help them make wise decisions. Remind them that God doesn't desert us when we face those problems where we need his wisdom most.

Keep in mind that even though these are biblical principles, they should be applied carefully, prayerfully, and advisedly. If you aren't sure how they apply to a specific situation, suggest that your friend consult a pastor or other counselor who better understands the particular problem.

BIBLICAL PRINCIPLES
TO HELP IN MAKING WISE DECISIONS

1. *God's authority rules supreme over all other authorities. Whenever we have to choose between obeying God or a human authority—whether that authority is set up in the church, family, military, or country—we should obey God.*

   All human authority is set up under God's ultimate authority and subject to him. Everyone fits into various places in various authority structures. You are subject to the rule of God's law to which all are held accountable; you are also under the governing authority of your national, state, and local laws. In the workplace, you may be the CEO who exerts authority over those operating under your leadership. Or you may work under the authority of a boss, who in turn may be under the authority of a supervisor. If you are in the military, you are additionally under the authority of those whose ranks are higher and subject to military law—which in some cases is more restrictive than civil law. In all situations, regardless of the authority structure that applies, you are not called to obey someone in authority who calls for disobedience to God. The Bible repeatedly tells us to obey God. Deuteronomy 13:4 says, "It is the Lord your God you must follow, and him you must revere. Keep his commands and obey him; serve him and hold fast to him." Deuteronomy 28:1–13 lists one blessing after another that will come to those who obey the Lord, including blessings for their children.

Jesus respected the position of authority held by the Pharisees (Jewish religious leaders who opposed him). Matthew 23:1–4 says, "Then Jesus said to the crowds and to his disciples: 'The teachers of the law and the Pharisees sit in Moses' seat. So you must obey them and do everything they tell you. But do not do what they do, for they do not practice what they preach. They tie up heavy loads and put them on men's shoulders, but they themselves are not willing to lift a finger to move them.'"

Look at Peter and John's response when commanded not to speak or teach in the name of Jesus after Jesus had told them to do just that. Acts 4:18–20 says, "Then they [the religious authorities] called them in again and commanded them not to speak or teach at all in the name of Jesus. But Peter and John replied, 'Judge for yourselves whether it is right in God's sight to obey you rather than God. For we cannot help speaking about what we have seen and heard.'" God gave his approval of their decision by continuing to work through them miraculously, which got them in trouble again. Acts 5:27–29 reports, "Having brought the apostles, they made them appear before the Sanhedrin to be questioned by the high priest. 'We gave you strict orders not to teach in this name,' he said. 'Yet you have filled Jerusalem with your teaching and are determined to make us guilty of this man's blood.' Peter and the other apostles replied: 'We must obey God rather than men!'" (italics mine).

2. *We are to look to the Lord as our ultimate provider.*

We can trust God to protect us and provide for all our needs. When people let us down, we should not despair. God stands ready to provide for us. We need to actively seek him and put our trust in him by praying for his help in specific terms.

Psalm 146:3–10 says,

Do not put your trust in princes, in mortal men, who cannot save. When their spirit departs, they return to the ground; on that very day their plans come to nothing. Blessed is he whose help is the God of Jacob, whose hope is in the LORD his God, the Maker of heaven and earth, the sea, and everything in them—the LORD, who remains faithful forever. He upholds the cause of the oppressed and gives food to the hungry. The LORD sets prisoners free, the LORD gives sight to the blind, the LORD lifts up those who are bowed down, the LORD loves the righteous. The LORD watches over the alien and sustains the fatherless and the widow, but he frustrates the ways of the wicked. The LORD reigns forever, your God, O Zion, for all generations. . . .

When your friend is in need, remind him or her to actively seek God and not to make decisions out of fear that there is no means of provision.

3. *Keep a clear conscience.*

God not only gives us external guidance through the Bible, but he also equipped each of us with a conscience. Your conscience works like a smoke detector, warning you away from danger. Sometimes your conscience will tell you not to do something that is not an outright sin but may appeal to a particular weakness in your character. When you respond to the warning signals your conscience gives, it continues to function well. This is why Paul said, "So I strive always to keep my conscience clear before God and man" (Acts 24:16).

Having a clear conscience is a good check that a particular decision would be OK. However, it is not the final test. You must still make sure the decision is within the bounds of morality laid out in the Bible. Paul also wrote, "My conscience is clear, but that does not make me innocent. It is the Lord who judges me" (1 Corinthians 4:4).

Bear in mind that our consciences are prone to becoming dulled if we override them time and again. Paul warned Timothy about false doctrine coming from false teachers. He wrote, "Such teachings come through hypocritical liars, whose consciences have been seared as with a hot iron" (1 Timothy 4:2). The book of Titus tells us, "To the pure, all things are pure, but to those who are corrupted and do not believe, nothing is pure. In fact, both their minds and consciences are corrupted" (Titus 1:15).

Therefore, we must take care that our consciences are kept in good working order by following their warnings. If we do not, we are left without a vital moral and spiritual warning system that can keep us out of trouble. If certain friends want you to tell them that something is allowable, when it may be questionable, direct them to consult their own consciences. But point out that their consciences may have become disconnected if they have repeatedly gone along with what they knew was wrong or gone against what they knew was right. Also remind them that God can restore a clear conscience and make it work properly once more.

The remedy for a malfunctioning conscience is found in the book of Hebrews:

> Therefore, brothers, since we have confidence to enter the Most Holy Place by the blood of Jesus, by a new and living way opened for us through the curtain, that is, his body, and since we have a great priest over the house of God, let us draw near to God with a sincere heart in full assurance of faith, having our hearts sprinkled to cleanse us from a guilty conscience and having our bodies washed with pure water. (Hebrews 10:19–22)

4. *Remember to ask God to guide you, then expect him to do so.*

When we don't know what to do, we do know the One who can give us direction. When we don't know what to do, we should actively look to God himself to be our guide. The explanation of how to do this is in chapter three.

5. *Use all that God has given you: intelligence, resources, support from your church, support from others who have been through what you are going through, common sense.*

We are to make the most of every resource God gives us. To whom much is given, much will be required. We are expected to use all the talents and resources at our disposal to do good with our lives.

6. *In the midst of whatever you are going through, remain thankful.*

Whenever you are struggling with what the will of God is in any situation, you can be sure God's will includes a thankful disposition. The Bible says, "Be joyful always; pray continually; give thanks in all circumstances, for this is God's will for you in Christ Jesus" (1 Thessalonians 5:16–18). You may recoil, thinking, *I can't be thankful for THIS!* But the verse doesn't say to be thankful *for* all circumstances. Rather it says to be thankful *in* all circumstances. You can be thankful *in* all circumstances only if you truly believe that the steadfast love of the Lord never ceases, that his mercies never come to an end (see Lamentations 3:22–23). We can only be thankful in dire situations if we "know that in all things God works for the good of those who love him, who have been called according to his purpose. For those God foreknew he also predestined to be conformed to the likeness of his Son, that he might be the firstborn among many brothers" (Romans 8:28–29). Regardless of what is happening—even things that no sane person would be thankful for—we can be thankful to God in such situations because he can help us overcome the bad with good.

APPLYING THESE BIBLICAL PRINCIPLES

Since these are principles, not pronouncements, encourage your friend to think them over and apply them in the following ways:

- In situations where you are not sure if or how these principles apply, pray for wisdom and for God to provide wise counsel in making important decisions.
- Seek godly counsel from your pastor and Christian professionals who have expertise in dealing with the kinds of issues you're facing.
- Get unbiased opinions by seeking out advice from reputable groups or organizations with regard to the issue, irrespective of who's involved.
- If you are in immediate danger, get to a place of safety first, then take time to sort out the issues with the help of wise counsel.

Overall, it is good to support your friends and give wise, godly counsel. However, as you move through whatever your friends are going through, look for opportunities to help them turn to God and the Bible to learn to make wise decisions for their lives. You can still be there to give your godly counsel, but they will be led into a closer relationship with God that will help them decide the right way to turn when you are not there to advise them.

CHAPTER NINE

Helping Friends
Even While They Are Disobeying God

A delicate situation presents itself when your friend is both going through hell and refusing to obey God in the midst of the situation. I spoke with Jill, whose longtime friend, Robin,* depended on her as a confidante during a difficult marriage. Robin and her husband were both Christians and attended church with Jill. As their marital problems grew worse, Robin decided to get a divorce. Jill warned against it, using the Bible to point out that Robin did not have scriptural grounds. Robin wouldn't relent. Jill felt frustrated, but continued to show love and concern for Robin while maintaining her position that the divorce was carried out in disobedience to God's Word.

After the divorce was final, Robin fell in love and shared her excitement with her friend Jill. But the man she was in love with was married. Jill listened and became deeply troubled to hear that Robin and her new love interest were sexually intimate. Jill confronted Robin with the fact that God considered their affair to be adultery. This time Jill swayed Robin. She told the man they could not have sex unless and until they were married. After his divorce was final, they married. They had not been married long when Robin's new husband was diagnosed with cancer. Jill stood by her

*Not their real names.

grieving friend, showing love and compassion to Robin and her husband as he was dying. Jill remained a faithful friend through the long illness, the husband's death, and Robin's seasons of grief and emotional torment. All the while, Jill offered both loving support and direction from the Bible.

Sometimes Jill was well received; other times she was rebuffed. She determined to stay beside her friend no matter what, but she paid a high price emotionally. She spoke of her own feelings of hurt and anger when Robin pushed her away or excluded her. There were times Robin was unwilling to obey what she knew to be God's decrees, times when she lashed out at Jill saying, "I don't want to hear any of your self-righteous garbage!" At other times she clung to Jill as her contact with God, seeking reassurance that God could truly forgive her for her sins. Whenever Robin turned back toward God, Jill always assured her of God's steadfast love and willingness to forgive. Whenever Robin turned away from God's will, Jill held out the truth of God's Word and lovingkindness. Jill is a good example for us all.

You may find yourself in similar situations, times when friends have gotten into a crisis by sin or when the anger and disappointments in life have caused them to throw in the towel morally. It is not unusual for anger and frustration over a life crisis to lead to a season of rebellion or outright disobedience to God. There may be times when a friend will come to you crying in repentance and times when someone becomes defiant against God and belligerent toward you as a Christian. While you should be willing to accept a friend who is angry, you should not be willing to accept abuse.

However, do not be surprised by the emotional and moral flip-flops that seem to link anger with a propensity to sin. Scripture warns us that anger can easily lead to sin if we are not on the alert. Psalm 4:4 says, "In your anger do not sin; when you are on your beds, search your hearts and be silent." This is echoed in the New Testament where it says, "'In your anger do not sin': Do not let the sun go down while you are still angry, and do not give the devil a foothold" (Ephesians 4:26–27). James wrote, "My dear brothers, take note of this: Everyone should be quick to listen, slow to speak and slow to become angry, for man's anger does not bring about the righteous life that God desires" (James 1:19–20).

Your friend will have to deal with anger in some way. And it's just a short jump from anger to sin. Your awareness of the bridge between anger and sin can help you help your friend to express anger while warning against the temptation to disobey God.

Also be on the alert for your own anger. We often react to hurt, frustration, or injustice with anger. Anger may be a protective mask for sadness or fear. It may be a way to try to gain power in a situation. When you find yourself angry at your friend, take time to examine the emotion to find its source. Ask yourself: Am I hurt? Am I frustrated? If so, what stands in my way, and what is the aim that is being frustrated? Is there some injustice that you are aware of that prompts righteous anger? Yes, even God himself gets angry at unfairness and injustice! Therefore, your anger can be right on behalf of your friend. Are you really sad about what is going on? Or are you afraid? The answers to these questions will help you manage your anger well so as to be of help to your friend.

If your anger springs from fear or an awareness of real danger, it can give you the boost you need to take action to help your friend. You may find yourself angry when you see your friend doing something that is obviously wrong because you know it is dangerous. This is normal and it is healthy to let your friend know how passionately you are concerned for his or her well-being. Perhaps this illustration will help you put your own anger into context.

When my son Taylor was nine years old, I watched him rollerblade down the driveway and into the street. He didn't notice the car that was rounding the corner, but from my vantage point, I did. He was only thinking of the fun he was having. I saw imminent danger. So I grabbed him and tackled him to the grass. He was shocked and thought I was angry at him. He was hurt and upset and demanded to know why I did what I did. It did appear that I was angry, and on the surface, I was angry in that moment. However, under the surface of my immediate—seemingly angry—actions was deep love, fear of what could happen to him, concern that he not get hurt, and a sincere desire to protect him. After I calmed down, I took Taylor aside and showed him the danger I had seen that he had not. I explained to him that I reacted in anger, but I only reacted so strongly because I care so deeply. I calmly explained why he must choose not to zip out into the street so close to a corner. It was only when I calmed down to examine and explain what was under my anger that he could see my loving concern.

When you first realize someone is about to do something clearly outside of God's will, you may get angry and come across as harsh. You may want to scream or do something drastic to make that person take pause. You may be genuinely alarmed that your friend has been deceived into thinking that God's Word doesn't mean what it says or that what it says doesn't really matter. And anger may be your initial emotional reaction. Just make sure that you calm yourself down enough to explain to your friend how passionately you care about his or her well-being and why you believe disobeying God will be dangerous.

SEPARATE LOVE FROM APPROVAL: LOVE THE SINNER EVEN IF YOU DISAPPROVE OF THE SIN

My friend Jill also provides a good example of how to love someone and offer support without compromising your position as one who speaks God's truth. The key is to speak the truth in love as we are told to do in Ephesians 4:15. It is possible to both speak the truth—even hard truth that rebukes sin—and continue to show love. In fact, the Bible says a true friend is willing take the risk of offering a needed rebuke. Proverbs 27:5–6 says, "Better is open rebuke than hidden love. Wounds from a friend can be trusted, but an enemy multiplies kisses." Jesus taught his disciples saying, "So watch yourselves. If your brother sins, rebuke him, and if he repents, forgive him" (Luke 17:3).

Some people think that they must withhold love until a friend chooses to obey God. But this is not what God does, and we are to imitate him. God continually loves us, provides for us, and holds out open arms to welcome any prodigal who returns home. He doesn't stop showing love, even though the person straying into sin and rebellion often leaves the place of God's love or is unable to receive the love God holds out. Therefore, I believe we are to continually express and display love for our friends—even while they are choosing to disobey God.

The way we convey our disapproval of sin is to speak the truth. You should clearly state your concern for a friend who makes decisions to do something sinful or becomes involved in sinful behavior. Make it clear that the Bible does not condone wrong behavior, therefore you cannot either. Also make it clear—to yourself and to your friend—that you know yourself to also be a sinner and you are dependent on God's forgiveness. Remind your friend that God gives us boundaries to protect us, that God's commands are given for our good, that God chastises us when we sin because he loves us and wants to correct us before we get hurt more or hurt others more. Emphasize God's willingness to forgive, redeem, and restore.

When you make your moral stance known verbally, also let your friend know that your disapproval of his or her behavior will not stop your love. Clearly explain that your display of love is not to be taken as an indication that you approve of any behavior that is morally wrong.

Rich Buehler, who used to be a Christian radio host, explained how to handle this kind of situation through the following scenario. He was often asked if a Christian should attend the wedding of a Christian friend or relative who was marrying a nonChristian against the clear dictates of Scripture. Rich told one such caller that he should sit down with his friend as soon as possible, present the scriptural case against being unequally yoked with an unbeliever, and urge the friend not to go ahead with marriage unless the fiancé converted. Then Rich told him to tell his loved one that he would attend the wedding. However, his attendance was not to be mistaken for approval of an unscriptural choice. Then, he advised the caller to buy the couple a nice gift and pray diligently for them. To me, this strikes the balance of what it means to speak the truth in love.

A word of warning is needed here. If your friend is suffering as a consequence of his or her own wrongdoing, beware that you don't see yourself as "the good one" and your friend as "the bad one." Some people will view you as a saint just for being a friend to someone who is reaping what has been sown. Taking on the role of "the good one" may make you feel superior, but it is a form of judging that is not true. It will undermine your friend's sense of self-respect, which will already have taken a hit and will destroy any growing trust in your relationship. I recommend taking the attitude given in Galatians 6:1, "If someone is caught in a sin, you who are spiritual should restore him gently. But watch yourself, or you also may be tempted." You are not above falling into sin, even though your friend was the one who fell in this round. Be gentle, not judgmental!

Your friend may also turn the tables on you and point out your areas of sin or disobedience—which we all have. The best way to deal with this is to be honest with yourself, your friend, and God. Don't try to say another's sin is worse than yours. Don't shy away. Instead, model the appropriate way to deal with sin.

The first epistle of John says, "If we claim to be without sin, we deceive ourselves and the truth is not in us. If we confess our sins, he is faithful and just and will forgive us our sins and purify us from all unrighteousness. If we claim we have not sinned, we make him out to be a liar and his word has no place in our lives" (1:8–10). If your friend points out an area where you struggle with sin or are out of line, simply agree. Say something like, "You are right. I do fall short in that area. Will you pray with me so I can confess that to God, ask his forgiveness, and have him cleanse me from that unrighteousness?" To make this work, you must be willing to turn from areas of known sin by the power of the Holy Spirit. If you are, tell your friend, "Thank you for pointing this out in my life. I believe I need God's help to overcome this just like you will need God's help to obey him in your situation. If you like I will pray with you to confess your area of temptation or sin, and ask God to give you the power you need to obey him in your situation."

There will be times when friends will ask for your advice when they are leaning toward disobedience to God's Word. If you are called on to give advice or be a sounding board, use the opportunity to try to persuade others to not be led astray by their own emotions or desires. Our culture says, "Follow your heart!" But the Bible points out that our hearts will lead us astray. Jeremiah 17:9 says, "The heart is deceitful above all things and beyond cure. Who can understand it?" Therefore, remind your friends not to follow their hearts, but to follow Jesus or follow the path of God's will.

This happens most often when life is painful. When we are hurting, it is very tempting to try to escape our pain in any possible way. The enemy of our souls is more than willing to offer all manner of "relief" that is sinful and dangerous to our spiritual and overall well-being but promises to temporarily numb us or distract us. You may find yourself in a position of having to warn a friend who is going through hell away from making choices that turn away from God's will and into paths of sin.

You are not responsible for another's choices, but you can make a strong appeal that your friend choose God's will no matter how hard it gets.

AT THE CROSSROADS BETWEEN GOD'S WILL AND SELF-WILL

When we come to the crossroads between our will and the will of the Father, it matters which path we choose! Being able to receive guidance from God only works when you are *willing* to do God's will. You don't have to be able to do it—because no one is able to apart from the power of God. What God requires is that we are *willing* to do his will, even when it opposes what we want. That is where we had better *choose* to take the path of God's will for us.

Isaiah described a path he called the "way of holiness." I see this as the path we take when we choose to follow Jesus in yielding to the Father's will for us. Isaiah wrote of this path, "No lion will be there, nor will any ferocious beast get up on it; they will not be found there. But only the redeemed will walk there, and the ransomed of the Lord will return. They will enter Zion with singing; everlasting joy will crown their heads. Gladness and joy will overtake them, and sorrow and sighing will flee away" (Isaiah 35:9–10)

Those who stay on the "way of holiness" will find "everlasting joy"; they will know times of "sorrow and sighing," but those will flee away. Instead of a ferocious beast overtaking them to destroy them, they will be overtaken by gladness and joy as they continue to follow God's path to the end.

Those who walk on this highway of holiness are specifically protected from the lion, who cannot assault them there. This imagery should be familiar. Peter warns all Christians, "Be self-controlled and alert. Your enemy the devil prowls around like a roaring lion looking for someone to devour. Resist him, standing firm in the faith, because you know that your brothers throughout the world are undergoing the same kind of sufferings" (1 Peter 5:8–9).

I see choosing to turn aside from God's will to follow our own as stepping off the highway of holiness, stepping away from the spiritual protection of God's clear moral boundaries. Wandering off the path of God's will leaves us open to the influence and evil power of Satan. And— make no mistake about this—he comes only to kill, steal, and destroy (see John 10:10).

The movie *The Ghost and The Darkness* tells the true story of a British officer who went to Africa in the late 1800s to oversee the construction of a bridge. He left behind his beloved wife who was pregnant with their first child. Construction was interrupted because of attacks by two lions who devoured more than 130 men. These man-eaters did not act like ordinary lions who killed for food. They seemed demonic and unnaturally bloodthirsty, terrorizing and attacking by day or night, undeterred by fires. They carried the human remains back to their lair where skulls and scattered bones were piled up like trophies. The natives called the two lions the Ghost and the Darkness, fearing the malevolent supernatural forces they seemed to embody.

The officer enlisted the help of a renowned game hunter and sought to kill the lions so the bridge could be completed. He saw the vicious attacks firsthand; in scenes too gruesome to describe, he saw men eaten alive. The delays caused by the lions made him unable to finish the bridge in time to return home for the birth of his first child. One scene in the movie depicts a dream he has while the lions are still on the prowl.

His wife and baby arrive unexpectedly to visit him in Africa. As the train pulls in, our view sweeps across the waving fields of golden grass. There, you can see the form of a lion moving speedily toward the train platform. A beautiful woman emerges, cradling an infant in her arms, both dressed in pure white. Crowds are running away from the station in fear of the lions. The officer is running against the crowds, toward his wife and child, yelling, "Go back! Go back!" She does not understand his urgency. She cannot hear his words distinctly above the noise of the running crowds. She smiles, expectantly, waving to him, holding the baby out for him to see.

The view shifts to the lion, gathering speed, hurtling through the grass, then to the officer. "Go back!" He shouts desperately. She smiles and hurries toward him. The lion bounds out of the grass, crushing mother and child to the ground, lustily devouring them before he can reach them or turn them back. Then he wakes up. It was only a dream in a movie. But to me it vividly portrayed what the Bible says Satan would love to do to any Christian he finds wandering outside the will of God— if given half the chance.

When I see people stepping off the highway of holiness, smiling because they think they are going to find relief from their pain, ease from their suffering, and the happiness that God's will has kept them from, I become like that man, crying out desperately to his wife. "Go back! Go back! Can't you see the lion?" If you have the chance, implore your friend to go back to the crossroads and turn onto the highway of holiness. Urge your friend and do your best to persuade him or her to stay in the protection of God's will. There may be sorrow and suffering for a while, but the road *will* lead to joy. However, if your friend is lured off that highway to do his or her own will instead of the Father's will, the lion who is seeking someone to devour will rush to pounce.

The following may help you explain the concept to your friend. There are only two paths leaving the spiritual crossroads where self-will crosses God's will. Jesus said, "If anyone would come after me, he must deny himself and take up his cross and follow me. For whoever wants to save his life will lose it, but whoever loses his life for me will find it" (Matthew 16:24–25). This tells us not only which path we are to follow, but also something about what the signs will look like at the crossroads. Taking the path Jesus took will look and feel like you are losing your life, but you will really be saving it. Taking the other path will *look* like you are saving your life, but you will really be losing it.

WHOEVER LOSES HIS LIFE WILL SAVE IT

Let's look at how Jesus made his choice that night in the garden of Gethsemane. Jesus never lost sight of his purpose, which he clearly stated when he said, "For I have come down from heaven *not to do my will* but *to do the will of him who sent me*" (John 6:38, italics mine). Jesus remained intent on doing the will of the Father. Throughout his life, his will was the same as that of the Father; he wanted what the Father wanted. But there came a moment, in the garden of Gethsemane as he approached the cross, when he was pressed beyond the point of having what *he* wanted agree with what his Father wanted. As a man, facing death, he could not make himself *want* to endure the shame and suffering he knew awaited him. At that point he came to a crossroads where he had to choose one or the other, his will or his Father's will.

This was not some dispassionate intellectual decision where Jesus simply knew what Scripture said and did it. He agonized about yielding his human will over to the Father. And yet Jesus' decision to *choose* the will of the Father over his own—despite the agony—is what led to his resurrection, glory, and eternal joy for himself and his followers. Matthew wrote that he was "sorrowful and troubled" (26:37). He needed his friends near him for support, telling his three closest friends, "My soul is overwhelmed with sorrow to the point of death. Stay here and keep watch with me" (26:38). He wasn't kneeling beautifully with his face gazing upward into heavenly light as we see depicted in stained-glass windows. The Bible says, ". . . he fell with his face to the ground and prayed, 'My Father, if it is possible, may this cup be taken from me. Yet not as I will, but as you will'" (26:39). He didn't pray just once; he prayed the same thing three times.

Mark records that he called his Father "Abba," which is the most intimate way a small child addresses his Father. He said, "Abba, Father, . . . everything is possible for you. Take this cup from me. Yet not what I will, but what you will" (14:36). Luke tells us that he was in such distress, "An angel from heaven appeared to him and strengthened him. And being in anguish, he prayed more earnestly, and his sweat was like drops of blood falling to the ground" (22:43–44).

When Jesus Christ had to choose between his will or the Father's, he was in agony. But once he made his decision and God handed him the cup of suffering he had feared, he didn't seek another path. He got up and willingly surrendered to those God allowed to arrest him. When one of his companions reached for his sword, Jesus rebuked him, and said "Do you think I cannot call on my Father, and he will at once put at my disposal more than twelve legions of angels? But how then would the Scriptures be fulfilled that say it must happen in this way?" (Matthew 26:53–54). His agony was incomprehensible, yet his choice was clear. He chose to have his life abide by the holy Scripture.

How could Jesus make such a choice? Scripture tells us, "Let us fix our eyes on Jesus, the author and perfecter of our faith, who *for the joy set before him* endured the cross, scorning its shame, and sat down at the right hand of the throne of God. Consider him who endured such opposition from sinful men, so that you will not grow weary and lose heart" (Hebrews 12:2–3, italics mine). Jesus could make this choice because he knew that the highway of holiness would wind through the sorrow and sighing but surely make its way to the everlasting joy that Isaiah prophesied.

Jesus wasn't choosing holiness *instead of* happiness; Jesus demonstrated that he believed true happiness—eternal joy—comes *through* obeying the will of the Father. Try to encourage your friend that the times of difficulty, trial, and pain can lead to something unexpectedly good up ahead. Jesus needed his friends during his dark night of the soul. Your friend does too.

WHOEVER SEEKS TO SAVE HIS LIFE WILL LOSE IT

God also gave us an example of another man, one who took the other path. This man also came to the garden of Gethsemane the night Jesus was arrested. But he didn't come to do God's will. He had come to do his own. He has a lot to teach us.

We dare not make Judas Iscariot such a one-dimensional villain that we lose the benefit of his example. Remember that he gave up everything to follow Jesus. He ministered alongside the other disciples for three years. He learned to pray, "Thy kingdom come! Thy will be done on earth as it is in heaven!" He had expectations of what Messiah would do when he came. It was only when the plan Jesus laid out made it clear that the way to the kingdom led through the cross that Judas had second thoughts. What Judas wanted and what God's will demanded were on a collision course, and he was not willing to turn aside from his will to do the will of the Father as Jesus had done. Judas chose, "Not God's will, but *mine* be done." Then he went to the chief priests and asked, "What are you willing to give me if I hand Him over to you?" (Matthew 26:15a). It's as if he figured that since he couldn't have the kingdom he anticipated, he might as well get some small measure of gain out of a plan that didn't go the way he had hoped.

Judas could not see how Jesus' crucifixion could possibly be the will of God. So Judas sought his own way to get something worthwhile out of his three-year investment. He gave up holiness to reach for the small measure of happiness he could buy with thirty pieces of silver. When Judas turned off the path of God's will, Satan was waiting for him. Sure,

Judas got the money. But he never got the happiness he thought it would buy him. Once he saw that Jesus had been condemned to death, he was seized with remorse. It's as if his eyes were opened and he saw what a fool he had been. He threw down the money and went out and hanged himself. Judas was dead before Jesus; but he did not share the joy of the resurrection or the glory to follow.

LESSONS FROM CHOICES MADE AT THE CROSSROADS

Let us learn from both Jesus and Judas by remembering the paths each chose. Jesus chose the highway of holiness. He denied himself what he wanted, and he went though tremendous agony to do so. When he chose to do the will of his Father, he had to die on the cross. But when he lost his life, he found it—he found eternal life and everlasting joy.

Judas followed the highway of holiness for a while; until it conflicted with what he wanted, what he expected of God. When he came to the crossroads where he had to choose either his will or God's will, he didn't deny himself. He sought to save his life; but when he tried to save his life by going against God's will, he lost it.

When people are going through extreme difficulties and trials, there will be times they have to choose whether to stay on the path of God's will or turn aside. You may have friends facing circumstances that seem too difficult, too traumatic to possibly be the will of our loving heavenly Father. That is when they may be tempted to turn aside from God's will to find some small measure of relief or pursue happiness down some other path. Their hearts and human reason may say, "Happiness this way!" That is when you can remind them that the human heart is deceitful and they dare not trust just what they feel or want. These are the times they will need courage to walk by faith and not by sight.

You can encourage them to trust the One who set up the signs in the Bible, a sure road map for our protection and eternal happiness. You can also help them recognize what the signs really mean and how to recognize them. The signpost saying, "God's Will" will appear to wind down into the valley of the shadow of death, through a dark night, and up a rugged hill to a cross, a place of self-sacrifice. But just over the hill dawns a bright new life that cannot be seen until one crests the hill. This is the path to everlasting life. It leads to fullness of joy in this life and the one to come. This path is guarded by God himself, our Father in heaven who loves us.

The signpost saying *"My Will Be Done!"* appears to wind away from the cross—avoiding the pain and shame it represents—and out into a lovely golden meadow where the winds of happiness beckon. But what we cannot see is the figure concealed in the golden grass of self-will. Our enemy lurks there, the evil one who roams about seeking someone to devour. The signpost beckoning toward self-will and away from God's will always leads into dangerous territory. It is deceitful, promising life by leading to death. Following the signpost of self-will "is a way that seems right to a man, but in the end it leads to death" (Proverbs 14:12).

Jesus had a good reason for wanting his friends and disciples to obey his commands as he obeyed the Father's commands. He said, "I have told you this so that my joy may be in you and that your joy may be complete" (John 15:11). The joy we find by remaining true to God's commands will make the experience of the cross—in whatever form we encounter it—worthwhile. You can encourage your friends with this hope as well.

While you cannot make good choices for others, you can demonstrate your concern and point out the markers on the "Highway of Holiness." You can warn friends not to be fooled by the detours into self-will that promise "Happiness: This Way!" You can gently point out how these diverge from God's revealed will and do your best to remind them that the "tall grass" of sin that sways so beautifully also conceals our mortal enemy. You can also pray, seeking God's protection from the evil one and for your friends to see the danger.

If your friends have chosen to disobey God and are facing the consequences, you should not say, "I told you so!" Neither should you step in to take the consequences for them or shield them. God built natural consequences for wrongdoing into the overall scheme of things to teach us to do right and avoid wrong. The sooner we learn that disobeying God brings pain, the sooner we will see God's laws as a protection for us and be more eager to obey. If you keep taking the consequences for others, they will not learn the correction God meant to teach.

While you can be a voice of truth, a source of prayer, and one who tries to warn others away from disobeying God while they are going through trouble, remember that God himself does not violate the free will he has given every human being. You cannot live a friend's life for him or her. The best you can do is to live your life in obedience to God by the power of the Holy Spirit. Let part of that personal obedience to God be showing your steadfast love and the grace of God to your friends even when they stumble or walk away from the "highway of holiness" for a time.

CHAPTER TEN

Going Through Hell Is a Process:
Prepare to Stay and Pray!

*I*mmediately after the killings at Columbine High School, while the people of Littleton, Colorado, were still dazed by the enormity of what had happened, the folks at *NightLine* had an idea. They would create a town meeting to bring together people of Littleton who had been touched deeply by the tragedy and people from Jonesboro, Arkansas, who had been through a similar tragedy thirteen months earlier. There two boys had ambushed teachers and students at Westside Middle School, killing four girls and a female teacher. In Jonesboro, the boys had been arrested. Perhaps there were lessons to be shared.

The promo for the special two-hour *NightLine* program suggested that the people of Jonesboro would offer comfort to those in Littleton. In my opinion, the program didn't have the anticipated effect. The shootings and bombings in Littleton seemed to reopen deep wounds in those from Jonesboro that were barely beginning to heal. Instead of a study in comfort for those freshly bereaved, it was a study in grief for all of us. The people of Jonesboro shared their ongoing struggles, heartache, pain, anger, and unrelenting sadness. The people of Littleton, watching via live satellite, shifted in their seats. Their somber expressions grew more so, if that were possible. As the folks from Jonesboro tried their best to bring hope, the reality settled in. They weren't anywhere near "over" their tragedy. They weren't going to be over it for a long, long time.

The people of Jonesboro were flesh-and-blood witnesses to the truth that life was not going to be back to normal in either town anytime soon. Some still seethed with anger, some openly wept over the ongoing loss of loved ones who were never coming back and deeds that could never be undone. Instead of gaining comfort, as intended, the people of Littleton seemed to lose hope before the watching world.

At one point, Ted Koppel seemed to be casting out a net for *any* hopeful comment that might encourage the audience from Littleton he had helped to assemble. One woman stood. I can't quote her word for word, but I clearly recall her point. She said, "Friends help." When asked what friends could do to help. She said, "It's not so much what they do. It's just that they stay. And they pray." Whatever your friends are going through, it's not so much what you do to help that matters; it's that you stay and pray.

Do not take for granted the steady comfort your friends can gain from knowing that you and others are lifting their names and their specific problems before God. There were times when our family was going through hell when I could not bring myself to pray. Months went by when the best I could do was cry and sob before God. My mind could not conceive a request or even a proper salutation. I was too confused by what God had allowed to happen. I was too upset to turn my soul's grief into sentences. But I did not worry at my lack of ability to pray. I knew without a doubt that our friends, Rayna and Larry, Kim and Rick, Betty, and many others whose names we did not know were praying faithfully for us. This gave us great comfort, not to mention the real help God provided through the answers to their prayers.

People need to know that there is someone in particular devoted to continually praying for them. I was impressed by a recent segment on a television news magazine that featured a group of Catholic nuns who raised money for a building project with their "Adopt-A-Sister" program. While brainstorming how they could raise funds for their worthy cause, a man suggested that they could offer a service that many people in today's society dearly need—prayer. It's not exactly a pay-to-pray arrangement. The donors contribute whatever amount they like to adopt a particular sister who devotes herself to pray for them. They can supply details of the names of the people in their families, the problems and needs they are facing, and issues that need prayer. Their adopted sister devotes herself to prayer on their behalf.

This program has been so successful that some people who don't even share their Christian faith have adopted a sister. One Jewish man spoke of how comforting it was to know that someone was consistently praying for his family. Another family became so attached to their eighty-five-year-old "adopted" nun that they gave her a birthday party. And those who participated saw many positive answers to prayer as well.

This goes to show how precious and powerful your commitment to pray for your friends could be. No matter what they are going through or how long it may take to get through hard times, you can make the process more bearable if you commit yourself to stay and pray. If you are committed to doing so, be sure to let your friends know. Just knowing can bring added comfort.

BE PREPARED FOR A WILDERNESS JOURNEY

When friends go through difficult times, there is a process involved. It may be likened to going through the wilderness or walking through a dark valley. If you understand some of the hallmarks of this process, you may be better equipped to be a good friend. Even though you may not be able to expedite the process, you can provide encouragement, and help your friends make it through with a good attitude.

Alcoholics Anonymous has a saying: "The only way out is through." That can be a scary thought if you have a friend going through a dark, uncertain, perhaps life-threatening, and scary experience. David wrote of the Lord, "Even though I walk through the valley of the shadow of death, I will fear no evil, for you are with me; your rod and your staff, they comfort me" (Psalm 23:4). On the deepest level, you cannot go through this valley with your friend. Only God can. But you can help your friend remember that God is there.

SET YOUR MIND ON GOD ABOVE

A while back I had to fly from Denver to Sacramento, and the forecast called for thunderstorms. Whenever I go to Colorado, I pray that I don't get caught in a thunderstorm. After takeoff, my sense of relief grew as we climbed through the clouds. The more time that passed as the plane flew heavenward without turbulence, the greater my sense of relief. The sunlight came shining into my window; the sky shone blue and bright in cloudless brilliance, so bright that I could not comfortably look out and up. But I love to look out the window whenever I fly, so I looked down and back toward the place from which we had come. There, far below, was an astounding sight that took me by surprise.

It was a thunderstorm, but such as I had never seen—even in pictures—because of my perspective. The plane must have been flying at more than thirty thousand feet through clear blue, cloudless skies. The clouds of the thunderstorm were so far below me that they seemed part of the ground. I could see the white tops of the clouds that faced heavenward and the edges of the dark gray underside that seemed to weigh them down. Lightning exploded across the whole bank of clouds, only occasionally breaking out to stab the ground. From where I sat, the scene appeared silent and beautiful. Only those on earth could hear the echoing thunder that accompanied the lightning.

A Bible verse sprang to mind: "And God raised us up with Christ and seated us with him in the heavenly realms . . ." (Ephesians 2:6). Now I could picture what that was like! Some time later the Lord showed me the following lessons from the sight he had given me the privilege of seeing. The storm represents the problems, trials, troubles, sorrow, peril, and suffering that come and go in our lives. God lives far above our storms, even beyond our universe. James calls God the "Father of the heavenly lights, who does not change like shifting shadows" (James 1:17). God remains as he was, is, and always will be. His light cannot be diminished by clouds that hover over the earth. He is light and the ultimate source of light. He is unchangeable. His steadfast love, his good intentions toward all who live on earth, his unapproachable brightness and shining goodness are always a reality. God does not change, even though our view of him often changes, depending on the storms that overshadow our lives.

God must surely look upon the storms in our lives from his position in the heavenly places, and we look at God from earth with our view of his goodness and love obscured by the storms. The difficulties, troubles, and suffering we endure can obscure his light from our lowly position. While we see only the dark underside of our situation, God can see the entire storm; he sees from whence it comes and where it will go. He sees the overall beauty and greater purpose the storm may serve. We can only trust that there is some greater purpose while our lives are shaken as if by thunder, and we may fear for our survival as one who fears that lightning may strike at any moment. And yet, the Bible tells us that God is not unfeeling toward those who dwell on earth. He sees every storm and does not send the storms to destroy us. Rather, God tells us how we can survive the storms of life by hearing and obeying his Word when the storms come (see Matthew 7:24–27).

Scripture tells us, "Set your hearts on things above, where Christ is seated at the right hand of God. Set your minds on things above, not on earthly things" (Colossians 3:1–2). We can obey this admonition by calling to mind the nature and power of God, who stands eternal, far above the difficulties that come and go from our lives. I see setting our minds above as remembering that God is always there and that he is always good. While we cannot know what storms may come, we can find reassurance if we know the heart of the one who promises to see us through life's storms. While we do not share God's foreknowledge of what will happen or how close the lightning will strike, we can trust that God knows what we do not. We can also trust that he will cause all things to work together for good to those who love him and are called according to his purpose.

Setting our minds on things above doesn't mean that we escape the difficulties that come in the normal course of life, any more than my recalling the thunderstorm I witnessed from the plane would keep me from getting wet if I stood outside during a storm today. The value of setting our minds above is that it gives us courage to do what is right in God's eyes when life is difficult and circumstances are threatening. Knowing that God is over all and sovereign gives us courage to go through whatever he allows into our lives. Setting your mind on God's unchanging nature will also make you a source of encouragement to your friends when the storms raging over their lives obscure their view of a loving God.

The reality of the view I had from where I was seated in "heavenly places" did not diminish the reality of the violence of the storm below. A man was killed by lightning in the area the day I saw the storm. Just knowing that God's love and good intentions shine brightly above while you are in the storm below does not mean that the storm is not dangerous. That danger is why we must not only know God as the One who is above, but we must also know God as One who is *with us* in the storm. We must set our minds above, and we must reach for God's outstretched hand to save us when our lives and our loved ones are in real trouble.

Those being ravaged by real and devastating forces crashing over their lives may need to be reminded that God is available to help them in the midst of their troubles. Psalm 107:6 says that the children of Israel "cried out to the Lord in their trouble, and he delivered them from their distress." Remember this and remind your friends to cry out to the Lord in the midst of their trouble. God is willing to deliver them from their distress although it will still be a process.

THE ONE WHO IS WITH US IN THE STORMS

Surely, Christ is seated at the right hand of God the Father. However, it is also true—and vitally important—that we know Jesus Christ as the One who came down from heaven to be *with* us in the storms of life. He did not just come and go. He preserved his place with us when he promised his disciples, "And surely I am with you always, to the very end of the age" (Matthew 28:20). He made this promise after his resurrection. Then he ascended into the heavens until the clouds obscured him from their view. Though they could not see him, the book of Acts shows how his followers maintained a close relationship with their living Lord. The Lord spoke to them; he worked with them by performing signs and wonders, he guided and directed them according to the need of the moment. They knew Jesus as the risen and ascended Christ, but they also knew him personally as one to whom they could turn whenever they were troubled and threatened by the storms of life.

When friends are going through the valleys and the storms come crashing down, it is important that they trust in God's unchangeable goodness and love. However, such storms have the potential of blocking our view of God, even though he remains sovereign in heaven. We must never forget that while God is eternal in the heavens, he has also made himself available to be with us always.

Think of Jesus' disciples who were out on the Sea of Galilee when Jesus came walking across the surface of the waters. Peter called out,

"Lord, if it's you, . . . tell me to come to you on the water."

"Come," he [Jesus] said.

Then Peter got down out of the boat, walked on the water and came toward Jesus. But when he saw the wind, he was afraid and, beginning to sink, cried out, "Lord, save me!"

Immediately Jesus reached out his hand and caught him. "You of little faith," he said, "why did you doubt?"

And when they climbed into the boat, the wind died down. Then those who were in the boat worshiped him, saying, "Truly you are the Son of God." (Matthew 14:28–33)

This wasn't even a major storm, but it was a walk of faith under extraordinary circumstances. And when Peter saw the wind-swept waves, he was afraid. There will be times when your friend is overtaken with fear even while walking in faith, and times when you may be afraid for your friend. Such fear is only human. When friends are going through such valleys and the storms come, there will be times when the circumstances are terrifying. Peter didn't begin to sink *spiritually;* his body actually plunged under the icy waters. In this *real* situation he cried out, "Lord, save me!" Then Jesus reached out his hand and caught him. Jesus didn't just lift him in some *spiritual* sense. He lifted him from the waters in which he might have drowned and put him safely in the boat. There may be times when a leap of faith precedes a plunge toward the depths, times a friend will have to cry out, "Lord, save me!"

The important thing is that your friend knows that Jesus is right there and that he or she will have the faith to call out to Jesus. When we do, Jesus will reach out and catch us. He will move in some real way to lift us out of the threatening circumstances. He will provide safety in some tangible form.

If your friend is a disciple of Jesus who has opened his or her heart to Jesus and received the promised Holy Spirit, remind him or her that Jesus has promised to never leave us or forsake us. If your friend has not yet received Jesus, encourage him or her to do so. Offer to pray and ask Jesus to come into your friend's heart, and help him or her to draw near to God to receive his strong hand of assistance. All we have to do is ask. Remind your friend that Jesus stands ready to help. He has the power to take our hands in *real* ways, to lift us up to a place of safety. And you can call out to him on your friend's behalf as well.

Storms will come and go, but they seem to come more often and with greater intensity when we are going through the valleys. You may wonder if it really matters whether we effectively hold on to heaven, seeking to hear and obey God's Word at a time when God may seem distant or uncaring. Indeed, it does. Jesus told a story that shows what makes the difference between survival and destruction in the storms of life. He said a foolish man built his house on the sand while a wise man built his house on a firm foundation made of rock. Then identical storms hit both dwellings. One survived; the other was destroyed. Jesus explained what made the difference, saying, "Therefore everyone who hears these words of mine and puts them into practice is like a wise man who built his house on the rock. The rain came down, the streams rose, and the winds blew and beat against that house; yet it did not fall, because it had its foundation on the rock. But everyone who hears these words of mine and does not put them into practice is like a foolish man who built his house on sand. The rain came down, the streams rose, and the winds blew and beat against that house, and it fell with a great crash" (Matthew 7:24–27).

Our willingness to hear and obey God's Word will make the difference between survival and destruction when the storms hit. You cannot control whether your friends hear and obey God's Word, but you can encourage them to do so.

KEEP A BROAD PERSPECTIVE
WHILE FRIENDS GO THROUGH THE VALLEYS

There is an advantage to the fact that you are not really going through the same valleys your friends are. You can keep a broader perspective, which allows you to help your friends look forward to a good future even while they can't see it yet. The prophet Jeremiah was not taken into captivity with the exiles of Judah, but his heart was with them in their captivity. He cared for them so much that he continued to seek God on their behalf. In his role as God's prophet, Jeremiah received a message from God for the exiles, which he sent along to them. He wrote,

> This is what the Lord says: "When seventy years are completed for Babylon, I will come to you and fulfill my gracious promise to bring you back to this place. For I know the plans I have for you," declares the LORD, "plans to prosper you and not to harm you, plans to give you hope and a future. Then you will call upon me and come and pray to me, and I will listen to you. You will seek me and find me when you

seek me with all your heart. I will be found by you," declares the LORD, "and will bring you back from captivity. I will gather you from all the nations and places where I have banished you," declares the LORD, "and will bring you back to the place from which I carried you into exile." (Jeremiah 29:10–14)

These people were facing seventy years in exile, but God allowed Jeremiah to put that into perspective. He was able to offer them hope in the midst of circumstances they hated. He was able to remind them that someday God would bring them out of what they were going through in captivity. Seek God on behalf of friends in trouble. You may not be able to get them out of the valleys God has allowed them to go through, but you may be able to pass along encouragement that God will bring them through with a future and a hope.

THE PHASES OF GOING THROUGH LIFE'S DIFFICULTIES

Those in the helping professions describe the process of getting through a crisis in various ways. What I present to you is a synthesis of what I studied as our family went through major crisis and the aftermath, the research I have done while interviewing people for previous books, and what I found to be true through personal experience.

In *The Crime Victim's Book*, Morton Bard and Dawn Sangrey identify three basic stages of crisis: impact, recoil, and reorganization.[1] The impact stage is when the person's safety is critical. The recoil stage is when the person needs the chance to express feelings, vent emotions, and have his or her feelings validated by people who care. The reorganization stage is when the person has to assess what has happened, decide how to deal with it, and prepare to go on with life in the future. These researchers note that these are rather fluid stages.

I see these three stages as valid although I describe them in different terms. The stages often overlap and are not experienced in a tidy progression. The process involves going through various aspects of these stages—off and on—for quite some time. But there will come a time when those in trouble will make it through these phases. When these phases are complete, you can be there to help your friends learn how to put the past behind them and get over what has happened.

PHASE ONE: AT THE ONSET OF THE CRISIS

When you see friends in trouble, your first inclination may be to try to help. But you may not be the best one to offer that help. When you have a friend in crisis, go immediately to God in prayer. Think of it like calling 911. In physical emergencies, you recognize immediately when you can't adequately help. Think of other kinds of crises in the same way. Step back and call on God for wisdom and help. If a friend is in imminent danger, don't put yourself in harm's way. It's better to call someone who is trained and equipped to help. If your friend were having a heart attack, you'd call an ambulance. If a friend were being physically abused by her husband, you'd call 911 or the police. You are not always the best person to come to the rescue. Figure out who is and call for help.

If there is no immediate danger, consider who could provide the resources your friend needs and encourage him or her to get help. If your friend is unwilling to get professional help, you might gather information that can help later, when he or she is ready to receive it.

The onset of the crisis is often the most dangerous time. If your friend, Mary, is unable to make decisions, you may want to assist her family in getting help for her and take decisive action in her best interests. Be careful not to overstep the proper boundaries. Ask the family if there is anything you can do to help in dealing with the crisis. Offer to care for her children while the family deals with the crisis. Offer to take care of some of the everyday concerns that become secondary during times of crisis, like preparing meals, answering correspondence, or cleaning the house.

If your friend (and her family) acts quickly to get help at the onset of a crisis, she can minimize the severity of the problems. Say she has lost her job after many years. If she settles into a routine of avoiding reentry to the job market, that can compound her sense of inadequacy. It can contribute to feelings of worthlessness that will be counterproductive. However, if she is encouraged to do something immediately to help herself prepare to reenter the job market, she might be more responsive the first week she's unemployed than she would after six months off the job.

Encourage Your Friend to Seek Professional Help When Necessary

Managing a crisis can be overwhelming. If professional help exists to deal with the kinds of issues impacting your friend and her family, encourage her to seek out someone who understands the issues. If she seems unwilling or unable, encourage her family or your mutual friends to find out what kind of help is available.

PHASE TWO: HELPING YOUR FRIEND THROUGH THE ONGOING DIFFICULTIES AND GRIEF

There's a surge of adrenaline that gets people through the onset of a crisis. They may still be in shock or denial, so they may not be fully aware of all the ramifications of what has happened. When people are fighting to survive, they are focused and energized. The toughest phase of helping your friend will come after the onset of the crisis has passed and before she can see her way clear to resume a "normal" life. This is what Morton and Sangrey called the recoil stage. This is the slow-motion time when it takes all of your friend's strength just to make it another day, when she feels like she hasn't made any progress. These are the days you will have to remind your friend not to "grow weary in doing good" but to trust that in due season she will reap good rewards if she doesn't give up.

When a major crisis hits, your friend won't get over it quickly. When someone drops a rock in a pond, the ripples don't stop until they extend all the way out to the edges. The rock here is your friend's crisis, and the pond is her whole life—her family, work situation, and even her faith and view of God. There will be ripples that go on for a long time. And God will be with her until the crisis and its myriad effects are gone, but this takes time. You can be a blessing if you are prepared to be a friend—on some level—all the way through.

PHASE THREE: HELPING YOUR FRIEND DURING THE RECOVERY STAGE

When whatever caused the initial crisis is over, there will be people who are wounded, relationships that are broken, and much that needs recovery or redemption. This is what Morton and Sangrey called the reorganization phase. Life has to be reassessed and reorganized to go on in light of whatever new realities have emerged. Your friend will need help to assess her situation and come up with a plan to work toward establishing a new way of life.

You cannot walk the road of recovery for your friend. But others have been down that road, and it may help to draw on their experiences to know what the process looks like and what pitfalls your friend might encounter. And it helps to know that others have come through triumphant. Having a plan, and the hope of others who've successfully gone before will help your friend persevere for the long haul in the aftermath of a crisis. If you have gone through something similar, share the comfort you have received from God as you went through your trials. If you have never had an experience like your friend's, you may be able to help him or her find others who have.

Encourage Your Friend to Seek Outside Support

Encourage your friend to find a support group. It may be a support group designed to deal with particular issues or a more generic group. Your friend may feel more comfortable just going out with a few other friends on a regular basis to talk through issues.

GETTING THE LAY OF THE LAND

One important part of what takes place during the recovery or reorganization phase is discovering the meaning of what happened. This is when your friend will think through the *Why?* questions. Your friend may need to reconstruct whole lifelong relationships in his or her mind to understand how new information fits with what was known before. Your friend will need to process how he or she feels and why, and grieve whatever losses he or she has had to bear. Part of the grieving process is to learn the lessons the valley had to offer. To whatever degree you can help your friend discover the meaning of what he or she has gone through or is going through, you will be doing a great service.

Sheldon Vanauken expressed his appreciation for how C. S. Lewis did this for him as he grieved his wife's death. In his book, *A Severe Mercy*, Vanauken wrote,

> C. S. Lewis was to be *the* friend in my loss and grief, the one hand in mine as I walked through a dark and desolate night. Other friends gave me love, and it was a fire to warm me. But Lewis was the friend I needed, the friend who would go with me down to the bedrock of meaning. I told him the insights that came to me through my grief observed—the title of the book he would write on his own future bereavement—and he gave me not only love but wisdom and understanding and, when necessary, severity.[2]

CELEBRATE THE MILESTONES
AS YOUR FRIEND MAKES PROGRESS

Whenever you see any signs of progress, celebrate. Take time and effort to recognize accomplishments and anniversaries. Remind your friend that there is a good future before him or her, however different it may be from the past. You can help in this regard by commemorating the positive milestones you see. In this way you can give him or her a new and brighter perspective.

When your friend is going through a prolonged difficulty, he or she will tend to lose perspective. Goals may be shot to pieces. Plans for the future may be irrevocably altered, and your friend may not be able to look forward with hope. Your ability to smile at the future is a gift you can give your friend when the time is right. Be sensitive to weep when your friend needs to weep, but also look for opportunities to help him or her begin to look forward. Ask God to show you how, and you may be amazed at the good ideas you come up with.

Let me share with you one of the ways I did this for my husband, Patrick, who is also my friend. Shortly after our ninth wedding anniversary, my husband shocked me by confessing that he had been unfaithful to me. In the year that followed, he went through hell. He was fired from his position as youth pastor; I was forced to resign my position in youth ministry at the same church. He had to give a public confession, lost his reputation, ended up working at a menial job, and we had a new baby to care for in addition to our young daughter. I wasn't sure how either of us would make it through the crisis phase, but we survived and so did our marriage.

Once the major life and death, marriage or divorce, *How are we going to make a living now?* decisions were made, life became a drudgery. But our tenth wedding anniversary was coming up. I realized that this could be the marker we needed to remind us that we were making some kind of progress when it felt as if we were getting nowhere—and didn't even know where our lives were headed. I prayed that God would give me an idea of how we could truly celebrate our anniversary and create some hope for the future.

This is the idea that came to me, which I carried out. I went through all of our photographs, from the time we were first dating, our wedding, the birth of each of our children, parties with friends, birthday parties, our trip to Israel, Christmas mornings, and the like. Then I assembled key pictures representing the course of our lives up to the point of the crisis, year by year. Then I left many blank pages, representing the uncertainty in which we were living. But on the last page of the photo album I put a photograph of a beautiful sunset. This was my photo history of our happy life together before the crisis and my assurance that we would have happy times ahead, that we would reach a happy ending.

I took this photo history with me when we went out to dinner. This was my surprise gift for Patrick. When we arrived at the restaurant, I put a tape of the Kenny Rogers song "Through the Years" into the car stereo. As the lyrics spoke of love lasting through the years, I turned the pages that depicted our love through the years for Patrick to see. As it ended with, "I'll stay with you, through the years." I turned the blank pages until I came to the sunset. That was my way of smiling at the future and reminding this man—my husband and friend—that we were making progress. It was one marker on the road as he traveled through the valley to remind him that he was headed somewhere, even though he couldn't see where that road led.

Don't fool yourself into thinking things will be back to normal next month. When you understand that this may be a long process, you can help your friend learn patience. Your realistic view of how long it may take to get through and your willingness to remain her friend can be of great help. Talk to others who have been through similar struggles. They'll help you get a realistic time frame. Then you may be able to help your friend think past survival to stabilizing, and past stabilizing to rebuilding a good life.

Yes, life can get so hard that your friend may forget there will ever be happy days again. Help him or her remember! Encourage your friend that a day will come when you can celebrate having made it through this valley. Let him or her know you're looking forward to the celebration.

Getting through hell is a process, and it may be a long one. Remember the wisdom shared by the woman from Jonesboro. It's not so much what you do, it's that you stay and pray that really helps.

CHAPTER ELEVEN

Waging Spiritual Warfare on Behalf of Your Friends

When friends are going through hell, it may be more literal than you realize. You may find yourself involved in a spiritual battle between the forces of good and evil that can be quite frightening when you realize this is not just a game or spiritual euphemism. The key to helping your friends is to stay with them all the way, trusting God to bring them through, and practice waging spiritual warfare on their behalf.

Let me suggest an analogy to underscore the importance of standing firm together against the powers of sin and darkness. It comes from the movie *Jumanji*. Granted, I know that this is a dark movie, but it paints a positive picture of how to deal with forces of darkness.

In the movie, two kids are caught up in an occultic "game" that unleashes demonic forces against them. The "game" sucks the boy into a dangerous jungle where he is held captive until someone rolls a certain number. The rules say that the only way to make the bad effects go away is to keep playing and finish the game. But the girl gets so frightened when the boy disappears into the game board that she runs away—she does not stand firm against the forces of evil. Twenty-six years later, another boy and girl are drawn into playing the game. They free the first boy (who has since grown into a man) and they find the first girl (now a woman) to complete the game. The forces of evil unleashed by the game can only be stopped if they finish that original game. In the process of being forced to combat demonic assaults together, the man and woman have to stand firm. They have to resolve the unforgiveness they hold toward each other. They also have the opportunity to "lay down their lives" for each other. He wrestles a crocodile to protect her and she jumps in front of a bullet that is meant for him. They keep playing the game to its end, even though they are terrified. They complete the game and all the demonic forces disappear, just as the rules state. All the evil that had been unleashed through the game is sucked back into the game. The bad that would have happened if they had given up never has a chance. They find themselves back in time, before it all started, yet with the knowledge of what has happened. The original boy and girl who played the game grow up, get married and share an intimacy, trust, joy, and appreciation for life that they never would have known if they had not battled the demonic forces together, stood firm, and won.

Here is the application for all Christians: Demonic forces and spiritual forces of wickedness are operative in our world. They can and will, at times, assail your life and your friends' lives. The only way out is to face the forces of darkness with the light of God, to meet their lies and deception with the truth of God's Word, and to persevere—standing firm against them—until the purposes of God are accomplished. In the midst of the conflict with demonic forces, you and your friends will find opportunities to demonstrate the love of Christ for each other and lay down your lives for each other. God could stop the assault at any time if he exerted his power over the forces of evil. Therefore, if he allows it to continue, even though you are asking him to remove it and waging spiritual warfare according to his instruction, that implies that he is developing your friends' endurance and perhaps yours too. You must determine to stand firm, to continue to resist evil until the demonic assault has run its course. You press on, being strong in the Lord. When the Lord brings you through, you will see that he is able to "work all things together for good" because you love him and are called according to his purpose. When you have been through this kind of conflict against the forces of darkness with friends or on behalf of friends, your friendship in Christ will be solidified and deepened. Your trust in the Lord will be strengthened too.

WAGE SPIRITUAL WARFARE
ON BEHALF OF YOUR FRIENDS

Regardless of what kind of "hell" your friends are going through, you can be sure that the forces of the evil one delight in their suffering and will be at work if allowed. Therefore, all Christians who are aware of the struggles your friends are facing should do their part to wage spiritual warfare on their behalf.

God has given you authority to wage spiritual warfare using the power and weapons of God. There may be times when you need to do this on your friends' behalf before more practical help will be welcomed. So if you find yourself caught up in fighting against friends and getting nowhere, or if they seem unable to grasp their needs or see their sins as sin, stop fighting and try fighting the enemy on their behalf. If the enemy has blinded them to some spiritual truth, just trying to make it clear to them won't work until the spiritual interference is put down.

Please don't skip this part just because you may not be familiar with spiritual warfare or you associate it with a particular segment of the body of Christ. Spiritual warfare cannot be left to those you consider superspiritual. The Bible tells us that we *are* in a spiritual battleground, whether we acknowledge it or not. When you become a Christian, you put on the uniform of a soldier of God. It's not a matter of whether you're in the battle, but whether you're wearing protective gear and wielding your spiritual weapons to advance the kingdom of God and beat back the forces of darkness. When friends seem to be down, you can make a difference by learning to wage spiritual warfare on their behalf.

As Christians we must begin with a basic understanding of the two conflicting spheres of power that operate in our world: God and Satan (also referred to in the Bible as the evil one, the deceiver, the father of lies, the thief, the devil, the serpent, and so on). We must never lose sight of the fact that God's purposes for us are always benevolent, and Satan's purposes for us are always malevolent.

When I use the phrase, "goes through hell," that is sometimes an apt description of the spiritual source of your friends' pain and suffering. Satan delights in causing pain, suffering, confusion, and discouragement in the lives of human beings made in the image of his arch rival. Jesus said of him, "The thief comes only to steal and kill and destroy; I have come that they may have life, and have it to the full" (John 10:10).

Some of the pain and suffering your friends go through may come directly from Satan and the spiritual forces of wickedness that are under satanic authority. The Bible says that Satan is the "god of this world." Therefore, many things that happen in this world that result in pain and suffering have their source in the forces of wickedness, ruled by Satan.

Jesus also pointed out the intent of the "thief"; he comes to kill, steal, and destroy. The thief opposes Jesus, who comes so that we may have life and have it more abundantly.

Each life is lived out in the midst of this basic spiritual conflict. If we understand the purpose of our lives and consider some of the difficulties people face in life, we will recognize the efforts of the thief who has set himself against God with the intent to thwart God's purpose.

Scripture says we are not to be ignorant of his schemes, so that we do not fall into his traps. At one point, Paul wrote, ". . . I have forgiven in the sight of Christ for your sake, in order that Satan might not outwit us. For we are not unaware of his schemes" (2 Corinthians 2:10–11). Again he wrote in a general letter to the whole church in Ephesus, "Put on the full armor of God so that you can take your stand against the devil's schemes" (Ephesians 6:11). This is not advanced Christianity but a basic awareness and stance for which all Christians should prepare themselves. This understanding is also a very powerful point from which to help your friends when the "hell" they are going through is influenced by the one for whom hell was created.

Knowledge of spiritual warfare can help you help your friends in two ways: (1) you can learn and practice spiritual defenses on their behalf and (2) you can share these things with your friends—if they are open to spiritual input—so that they too can begin practicing spiritual warfare in the midst of their troubles. In this case, you can agree to fight the enemy of your souls side by side.

BASICS OF SPIRITUAL WARFARE

Let's look at the basics of spiritual warfare that will help you, even if this is entirely new to you. This is not something you should approach lightly; it's not some magic trick you can learn to amaze your friends. In the book of Acts, we see Paul and the other disciples driving out demonic forces in the name of Jesus. It looked easy enough, so others decided to try it. We find this account in Acts chapter 19:

> Some Jews who went around driving out evil spirits tried to invoke the name of the Lord Jesus over those who were demon-possessed. They would say, "In the name of Jesus, whom Paul preaches, I command you to come out." Seven sons of Sceva, a Jewish chief priest, were doing this. One day the evil spirit answered them, "Jesus I know, and I know about Paul, but who are you?" Then the man who had the evil spirit jumped on them and overpowered them all. He gave them such a beating that they ran out of the house naked and bleeding. (vv.13–16)

Rule number one, you and I have no power to do battle with the enemy of our souls apart from Jesus Christ. As members of the body of Christ on earth, we have authority from Jesus to conduct spiritual warfare in his name. It's as if God has given you a court order that allows you to take back in prayer whatever the devil has stolen. God has deputized you with authority to arrest the evil work of the devil in the lives of others and in your own life. To do this, you pray in the name of Jesus, commanding whatever forces of evil may be in operation to stop their assault. Pray the promises of God, affirming that God's Word is true, and trusting God to apply his Word to those for whom you pray. When you see that the devil has come in as a thief to steal, you can pray that God will restore what the thief has stolen. You don't have personal power to do this; you have been given authority by the power that is in Jesus, who was given all authority in heaven and earth when he defeated Satan by dying on the cross. You can invoke that authority on your friends' behalf and trust God to sort out how much of what is happening in their lives is as the result of spiritual forces of darkness.

One word of warning here, don't get into prescribing what you think is "of the devil" as though those who are suffering are somehow in league with the devil. You can pray that God counteract any forces of the evil one at work against your friends without assaulting your friends. There are many reasons people suffer. Sometimes well-meaning friends will decide that the suffering is the result of some association with the evil one and shun those who are suffering or demand that they pray harder or renounce unconfessed sin. You are not the Holy Spirit; let the Holy Spirit guide your friends into all truth about spiritual things. You can do harm if you accuse people of somehow siding with the evil one just because they are suffering in ways you cannot understand. Remember Job's friends.

PROTECTIVE COVERINGS AND SPIRITUAL WEAPONS

Ephesians 6:12–18 lays out how the Christian is equipped by God for spiritual warfare. The verses are in bold. Here are the basics taken from that passage of Scripture:

1. *Recognize that our battles take place within an ongoing spiritual battle.*
    "For our struggle is not against flesh and blood, but against the rulers, against the authorities, against the powers of this dark world

and against the spiritual forces of evil in the heavenly realms." We approach this issue by recognizing that we are already in a battle.

2. *God issues protective gear. It's our responsibility to put it on and use it.*

"Therefore put on the full armor of God, so that when the day of evil comes, you may be able to stand your ground . . ." God provides spiritual armor that will protect us. It is our responsibility to put it on and to stand our ground. This isn't done automatically.

3. *There will be times you will have to stand your ground against the forces of darkness.*

"and after you have done everything, to stand. Stand firm then, . . ." If friends are besieged in a spiritual battle, there may be times you will need to stand firm spiritually with them against any unwholesome or untrue influence of the enemy that can sway their thinking until their minds are renewed in agreement with God's Word. This takes persistence, but it pays off. When you take a stand with a determination not to give up until the power of false and/or sinful beliefs loses its influence over your friends' minds, you will see spiritual progress.

4. *Truth holds all the other protective armor in place.*

"with the belt of truth buckled around your waist, . . ." The armor familiar to the people who read this letter originally was the armor of the Roman soldier. The centerpiece of his armor was the belt, to which all the other pieces attached. So, too, truth must be the centerpiece of your spiritual covering. You must know the truth of God's Word. You must trust Jesus Christ who called himself the Truth. You must judge all by whether it is true. Anything that is deceptive, that shades the truth or diminishes the truth in any way, is not how God will protect you. Take refuge in the truth. Test everything by whether it agrees with the truth revealed in the Bible.

5. *Make sure you have the righteousness of Jesus firmly in place.*

"with the breastplate of righteousness in place, . . ." The breastplate covers the heart, a soldier's most vulnerable area. So, too, your heart must be protected with the strong assurance of your righteousness—not how righteous you are by doing good, but the unassailable righteousness of Jesus that is yours by faith in him.

Whenever you begin to pray against the forces of the devil, he will go for your heart. He will remind you of things you have done wrong that he hopes you will believe disqualify you from praying in the full authority of Jesus Christ. This is not true and you must not fall for such a lie. The apostle Paul, who wrote the letter to the Ephesians instructing them about spiritual armor, is the same one who wrote, ". . . that I may gain Christ and be found in him, not having a righteousness of my own that comes from the law, but that which is through faith in Christ—the righteousness that comes from God and is by faith" (Philippians 3:8b–9). Your breastplate of righteousness is nothing less than the unassailable righteousness of Jesus Christ himself. That is what protects you as you do battle.

6. *Be ready to move out with the protection and support of the gospel.*

"and with your feet fitted with the readiness that comes from the gospel of peace."

7. *Hold up your assurance that God will keep his word.*

"In addition to all this, take up the shield of faith, with which you can extinguish all the flaming arrows of the evil one." Soldiers of old didn't just want to wound one person with each arrow. They shot flaming arrows so that each arrow would not only wound but also destroy everything around it if the flames found something that could catch fire. Your faith can be like a Roman shield, which could be dipped in water so that when the arrows hit, they could neither kill the initial target nor spread their flames.

Be sure that Satan is not satisfied to wound one victim at a time. The arrows that are aimed at your friends' lives blaze with flames of hell that are meant not only to wound them but also to destroy as much as possible in your friends' life, families, finances, and the lives of their children. Therefore, you must know how to use your faith in the truth of God's Word to stop those fiery missiles whenever they come near, whether they are aimed at your friends or yourself.

Whenever the attacks come, and in whatever form they take, you must meet them with absolute faith in God's promises and the truth of God's Word. If you have to choose whether to believe a fear that you will run out of money or God's assurance that he will provide, affirm that God has promised to take care of you. If you feel condemned for some sin that is already confessed and forgiven, don't let that wound your heart. Instead, thank God that you have already been forgiven as promised in his Word. If you are induced to hold a grudge or refuse to forgive a friend for some sin he or she committed but has since confessed and repented of, don't go along with the unforgiveness that is clearly wrong. Instead, thank God that your friend is forgiven, and affirm your choice to forgive as well. Act on God's Word. Hold it up in prayer by stating that you believe it.

8. *Let your assurance of salvation protect your mind.*

"Take the helmet of salvation . . ." The helmet protects the head, and salvation protects your mind. The Bible says, "Therefore he [Jesus] is able to save completely those who come to God through him, because he always lives to intercede for them" (Hebrews 7:25). We must know, understand, and be sure in our minds that Jesus brings salvation. That salvation involves being saved for heaven, but it also means being saved from the power of sin and being saved from the rule of Satan in everyday life.

If this is not your assurance, I encourage you to fill your mind with God's Word that addresses the full salvation God promises his children. When you see the salvation God promises, you will see wherever the enemy may be keeping your friends from enjoying that full salvation. With the assurance of knowing what God intends, you can discern intelligently how to pray for your friends' specific needs.

9. *Your only offensive weapon is the Word of God.*

"and the sword of the Spirit, which is the word of God." Look at how Jesus did battle with Satan when he went through his temptation. Three times the devil tried to trick him, and three times Jesus replied, "It is written. . . ." Jesus did not argue with the devil. He simply used the

Word of God—which he knew by heart—to combat the deceptive suggestions of Satan.

The Bible says, "Do your best to present yourself to God as one approved, a workman who does not need to be ashamed and who correctly handles the word of truth" (2 Timothy 2:15). Since the Word of God is our only offensive weapon, we need to know how to handle it. When I was a youth pastor, a boy named Kevin showed up at youth group with a real, sharp, two-edged Samurai sword. He had no idea how to handle it and therefore posed a great danger to everyone nearby. It's the same way with us and the Bible. God's Word is living and active; it's powerful. And if we don't take time to learn how to handle it, we can be dangerous.

Learn the basics of the Bible. Learn how it applies to your life and your friends' lives. Never use Scripture to try to put someone in his or her place. Rather, learn to use God's Word as a weapon against the enemy of your souls in a way that benefits others.

10. *Stay alert and keep on praying!*

"And pray in the Spirit on all occasions with all kinds of prayers and requests. With this in mind, be alert and always keep on praying for all the saints." Notice the stress here is not on how you pray but that you *keep on praying.* It is as you keep on praying for your friends that the Holy Spirit will direct you regarding how you might conduct spiritual warfare and pray on their behalf. Just keep on praying.

Sometimes, the best way you can help your friends is to go directly to the Lord and pray, even though it may seem like a circuitous route. Holding on to heaven implies that you are one who will go boldly before God's throne of grace to find help for your friends in their times of need. Here are some insights on how you can pray every day and wage spiritual warfare on your friends' behalf.

DON'T NAG YOUR FRIENDS;
NAG GOD ON THEIR BEHALF

When you see areas in your friends' lives or attitudes that need to change, you may be tempted to nag about them. If you're the kind to nag, that's OK, but don't nag your friends. Instead, nag God on their behalf. Jesus described a widow who had been treated unjustly. She wouldn't stop pestering the judge until he gave her what she wanted. Jesus said it's good to pray like that, to persist until God answers. If you turn every temptation to nag your friends into a prayer for them, you will surely see better results. Seek the Lord to help your friends; that will have a better effect than trying to change them directly.

DON'T WORRY ABOUT YOUR FRIENDS;
TURN EVERY WORRY INTO A PRAYER REQUEST

It's not unusual to worry when your friends are going through troubles. You can worry, but that won't do your friends or you any good. Besides, it is direct disobedience to the Word of God and Jesus' commands. Jesus recognized our tendency to worry and counteracted it. He taught, "So do not worry, saying, 'What shall we eat?' or 'What shall we drink?' or 'What shall we wear?' For the pagans run after all these things, and your heavenly Father knows that you need them. But seek first his kingdom and his righteousness, and all these things will be given to you as well. Therefore, do not worry about tomorrow, for tomorrow will worry about itself. Each day has enough trouble of its own" (Matthew 6:31–34).

You don't have to let worry consume you as you consider what your friends are going through. Rather, you can help them tremendously if you choose to let worry lead directly to prayer. The Bible treats worry as a choice, not as something you cannot help. If you constantly worry, that's not your personality; it is a practice God can help you change to others' benefit.

Here's how. The Bible says, "Do not be anxious about anything, but in everything, by prayer and petition, with thanksgiving, present your requests to God. And the peace of God, which transcends all understanding, will guard your hearts and your minds in Christ Jesus" (Philippians 4:6–7). God's promise of peace is made to those who choose to turn worries into requests to God. Think of it as creating a requisition to fill a specific need in your friends' lives, then give that requisition to God. Your worries are already itemized in your mind. Just turn each into a request, speak it or write it out to God, then thank him that he will take care of it. Repeat this process every time the worry comes to mind. There is an added benefit to this practice. You will not only see God's provision, but God also promises the peace that passes all understanding to those who practice not being anxious.

You may also help your friends by encouraging them to turn their worries into prayer. Make a pact that when you catch each other worrying about anything, you will turn those worries into prayers that you will pray together. This works. Choose to believe God's promises of provision. When we were going through hard times, friends did this with us, and we saw that God always sent what we needed when we needed it. Encourage your friends to tell God every single thing they need; everything that could be a worry can just as easily become a prayer. This simple practice can do your friends good directly when prayers are answered and indirectly when their hearts and minds are guarded by the peace of God.

PRAY SPECIFICALLY, CONSISTENTLY,
AND SECRETLY FOR YOUR FRIENDS' NEEDS

If your friends need your help, they probably don't need a sermon—at least not just a sermon. They do need you to believe God enough to pray for them. Jesus said, "When you pray, go into your room, close the door and pray to your Father, who is unseen. Then your Father who sees what is done in secret, will reward you" (Matthew 6:6). You have the inside scoop about your friends' struggles. Never use that information to dishonor them before others; but don't waste it either. Use it to shape specific prayers. To keep me focused, I use blank journals to write my prayers. I recently reviewed these prayers from the times when my husband—who is also my friend—was going through his darkest times. I was amazed as I saw the specific requests I made secretly that have been answered for all to see. Pray for your friends; pray persistently and pray in secret.

KEEP A BALANCED VIEW

A word of warning may be in order here. God is a God of balance. While he does not want us to be unaware of the devil and he wants us to be prepared to go to battle fully dressed and fully armed, there is another common trap to guard against: that is to become focused on Satan and the forces of evil instead of focusing your attention on the Lord and his kingdom.

I have a friend who just discovered the power we have to do battle against the devil. She quickly reinterpreted every facet of her life struggles and her friend's struggles to be a trick of the devil himself. That is not the whole picture. While the forces of evil may influence and delight in every sinful and hurtful thought or deed that takes place on earth, they don't necessarily deserve direct credit. The Bible tells us that human beings are influenced by the world, the flesh (our own sin-inclined nature), and the devil.

There's plenty that can go wrong just by yielding to the influence of the world and our own nature, without the forces of evil having to raise a finger—if they have fingers!

Don't give the devil more attention than he is due. Be aware of the possibility of satanic influences. Learn to pray against them, take authority over them, and deal with them according to how God says we should. But don't look for a demon behind every bush. If you believe that your friends' issues are somehow tied up with occultic forces or that they are in some kind of bondage to spiritual forces of wickedness, seek out prayer support from those in your church community who are better equipped to deal with this kind of thing. You may also want to better educate yourself on the subject by reading good books, such as *The Bondage Breaker* by Neil Anderson.

Be on the alert for the devil, but don't get out of your secure position in Jesus and don't get sidetracked to chase the devil down. Let me illustrate what I mean by sharing something that happened to me. Recently, I was driving in a hot and dry rural area toward a house where my children were playing outside. As I drove up the dirt road, I happened to run over a rattlesnake. It kept slithering along in the direction of my children. Once I saw that it was still moving and that it was indeed a potentially deadly rattlesnake, I backed my car over it, then tried to hit it again going forward. It slithered off into the grass, wounded, but alive. Now, I did all of this from the safety of my car.

That's a pretty good picture of how I approach the enemy. I know he's in the grass. I know he'd strike and try to kill me in an instant if I stepped out of my covering in Christ and came after him apart from my position in Christ. The danger would be the same whether I tried to engage him to protect someone I love or I just wandered off the "highway of holiness" that God has established for me. So I don't go looking to pick a fight with the devil. I trust that as long as I stay abiding in Christ, just like I stayed in my car against the snake, I can remain protected and can strike a blow against the forces of evil whenever I see them at work against someone I love. If I happen to encounter satanic opposition, if the forces of darkness get in the way of where the Lord is taking me, I use all the power of Jesus at my disposal to do as much damage as I can. I use the power and prayer privilege God has given me to stop the evil one from getting near my loved ones, and if I see him moving that way, I use the power of God to drive him away.

I don't focus my attention on looking for demons under every rock. I focus my attention on seeking first God's kingdom and his righteousness, and the work God has given me to do each day. But I am not ignorant of the devil's schemes, and when necessary, I meet him in Christ. If I approach him in my own strength, I am overwhelmed with fear and at great risk. If I approach him in Christ, I may still feel afraid, but I am protected and can deal with him directly if he comes across my path.

Therefore, I urge you to be prepared to help your friends in many ways. Provide practical help, emotional support, and spiritual help. When friends are "going through hell," they will need all the help they can get. The help you have to offer needs to come from One whose strength is greater than yours, whose love is limitless, whose wisdom is higher. That is why you need to continue to hold on to heaven. As you do, God himself can work through you to help your friends.

CHAPTER TWELVE

Dealing with the Emotional Ups and Downs

*L*ong ago a woman moved away from her homeland because times were tough. She, her husband, and their two grown sons relocated in a neighboring country where they hoped to make a better future for themselves. They settled down. The two sons married and the woman looked forward to having grandchildren she and her husband could love and coddle in their old age. But life took a tragic turn for this woman's family.

Her husband died. Shortly thereafter one of her sons died. Then her only remaining son also died. Her hopes and dreams for the future died with them. She had never held a paying job, had no insurance, and had no idea how she would survive in a foreign country without family or friends. So she decided that she must return home.

She had been raised with faith in God, but how could God allow such overwhelming tragedy to befall her? Surely God could have spared any one of the men she loved, or all three, but he did not intervene. If she had not believed in God, she would have had no one to blame. As it was, she did believe, and she blamed God.

One of her daughters-in-law insisted on remaining with the woman, even though she was despairing. The young woman accompanied her mother-in-law back to her hometown of Bethlehem. The woman's name was Naomi; her daughter-in-law was Ruth, whose story is recorded in the biblical book of Ruth. Listen to the reply Naomi gave the friends who greeted her when she returned.

> So the two women went on until they came to Bethlehem. When they arrived in Bethlehem, the whole town was stirred because of them, and the women exclaimed, "Can this be Naomi?"
>
> "Don't call me Naomi," [which means pleasant] she told them. "Call me Mara, [which means bitter] because the Almighty has made my life very bitter. I went away full, but the Lord has brought me back empty. Why call me Naomi? The Lord has afflicted me; the Almighty has brought misfortune upon me." (Ruth 1:19–21)

You'll notice that no one ventured to correct her attitude. When people have suffered terrible losses, it does no good to argue with their feelings. Actually, Naomi was right; she had gone out full and come home empty. She had gone away a pleasant woman and come home embittered. Ruth gives us a good example to follow when those we care about are suffering and expressing their emotions, even blaming God out loud. Ruth stayed with Naomi and loved her.

Naomi didn't need a pep talk or a sermon or someone to chide her. She needed someone to stay with her until God redeemed her losses and restored her hope. The story goes on to show us how God sent a kinsman redeemer, a near relative named Boaz who was willing to buy Naomi's son's property, marry his wife, and raise up children in his name. Boaz fell in love with Ruth; they married and had a child. Naomi lived to hold her grandson in her once-empty arms. "Then Naomi took the child, laid him in her lap and cared for him. The women living there said, 'Naomi has a son.' And they named him Obed. He was the father of Jesse, the father of David" (Ruth 4:16–17).

Ruth stayed with Naomi through her emotional ups and downs. She stayed with her when she was pleasant and when she was bitter. She stayed with her when she was blaming God and bemoaning how he had allowed her to lose it all. She stayed with her until she saw God redeem all that was lost in ways they couldn't fully appreciate until God brought them to pass. Naomi, who had become bitter toward God at her lowest point in life, became the great-, great-grandmother of King David and a woman in the lineage of Messiah.

When your friends are going through hell there will be times when they blame God, times when they are bitter, times when they rant and rave about how a supposedly loving God could let such things happen to them. Don't think you have to defend God. God can take care of his own reputation by proving himself the ultimate redeemer. Just stay by your friends through their ups and downs. Listen while being respectful of their great losses and terrible pain. Pray for God to send real redemption in a tangible way. There may be times when you can help them weed out roots of bitterness, but be quick to listen and slow to speak. Wait on the Lord with them. Then when God moves to redeem their losses, celebrate with them too!

As you experience emotional ups and downs with your friends, remind yourself that human emotions are not right or wrong; they are expressions of what is going on within. The Bible is full of real people who experienced and expressed all manner of human emotions. The notion that Christians only experience, only feel, or should only express certain emotions is not true or helpful. While the Bible does stress that we should control our emotions instead of allowing them to control us, it does no good to deny them. Rather, recognizing all emotions and finding their sources can bring understanding that will help you and your friends. All feelings can cause us to turn to God and seek him to gain self-control.

This chapter will help you understand some of the emotional sway your friends may go through. I hope it also reminds you that your emotions will fluctuate as you support your friends. That is normal and to be expected. Be sure to address your emotions and allow them to drive you into the arms of God when you need comfort or encouragement yourself.

One act of service you may provide for your friends is to allow them to vent their feelings as they try to deal with their challenges, grieve their losses, or process whatever they are going through. Following are some of the common emotions they are sure to experience at some point.

ANGER

Anger will emerge at some point in any life crisis or season of difficulty. You will have the opportunity to help friends process their anger in healthy ways. However, you must understand that anger itself is not bad. It is a God-given emotion that is part of the stamp of God's image in our nature. God himself gets angry, and therefore, human beings have the propensity to be angry as well. If you appreciate anger as a normal part of processing the challenges of life, you will be better able to help your friends deal with their anger in appropriate ways.

The Bible does not say, "Don't be angry." It says, "'In your anger do not sin': Do not let the sun go down while you are still angry, and do not give the devil a foothold" (Ephesians 4:26–27). So when friends go through something that stirs up anger, be willing to listen. Also, be alert to where the ways your friends deal with anger may cross the line to become sinful behavior.

Dave Dravecky, the former pitcher with the San Francisco Giants who lost his pitching arm to cancer, had to deal with anger as part of what he went through. He and his wife Jan now help others through the Dave Dravecky Outreach of Hope. In their newsletter, Dave addressed the importance of friends and caregivers who will not turn away from the suffering person just because he or she is angry. He wrote,

> When you accept anger for what it is and give a person permission to be angry—not permission to be abusive or to remain locked in anger, but permission to experience that emotion—you open the door to a relationship where you can discover the hurt, frustration, or fear that lies behind the anger. Then you can begin to talk about it, which helps

in the journey of pain and suffering. When there is an acceptance of anger a person instinctively knows, *I am dealing with someone who is safe.* This is a relationship that is safe. Then the person can be much more open in saying, "Here is what is behind my anger. It is too scary, too difficult for me to deal with on my own." . . .

There is great freedom in knowing you can share your deepest thoughts and deepest fears with someone who accepts you and, in the process, gives you the encouragement to cope. No one wants to stay angry. The goal is to move from a place of anger, which keeps us from dealing with what we're up against, to a place of peace and contentment that comes from effectively communicating what's really going on inside.[1]

The Bible does not say that anger is a sin. There are plenty of times God is angry; we even see times Jesus got angry; so there are times anger is warranted. However, we are also cautioned that anger can cause us to sin and must be dealt with daily.

Anger will sprout up. If your friends never experience or express any anger, they may need help or permission to acknowledge those feelings. Anger needs to be recognized and expressed in a way that is not an act of sin. Anger can be expressed verbally, or in writing, or in some other way that does not harm anyone. It's OK for anger to sprout up, but it's not OK for it to go underground and set roots.

Ephesians 4:31 says, "Get rid of all bitterness, rage and anger, brawling and slander, along with every form of malice." Once anger is recognized, we are to aim to get rid of it. However, we are not condemned for feeling angry. In the process of getting rid of the anger, we also will come to understand some of what God has to teach us in the situation. The process of ridding ourselves of anger is a process that brings purification.

BITTERNESS

We are also told to get rid of bitterness. Hebrews 12:15 says, "See to it that no one misses the grace of God and that no bitter root grows up to cause trouble and defile many." Bitterness or resentment can be seen as anger that has gone to seed. It becomes like a weed in one's soul that sends out creeping roots. If we deal with anger initially, it has no chance to turn into bitterness. But if it is nursed or left alone, anger will turn into a resentment that can take over a person's life and spread out to hurt many other people.

In the book of Acts we see Peter and the other apostles dealing with a man named Simon. When Simon saw the power of the Holy Spirit imparted to those upon whom they laid their hands, he offered them money to give him the same power. But "Peter answered: 'May your money perish with you, because you thought you could buy the gift of God with money! You have no part or share in this ministry, because your heart is not right before God. Repent of this wickedness and pray to the Lord. Perhaps he will forgive you for having such a thought in your heart. *For I see that you are full of bitterness and captive to sin*'" (Acts 8:20–23, italics mine).

Peter was able to discern bitterness in Simon's heart and that he was captive to sin. Simon then begged Peter to pray for him to change and be spared God's displeasure. When you see a root of bitterness spreading in a friend's heart, dare to point it out. Do so kindly, but quickly. Bitterness has a tendency to spread. The longer it is left in a person's heart, the more difficult it is to eradicate.

The right way to deal with anger is to confess it and ask God to help you get rid of it. You may need to go to the people toward whom the original bitterness was felt and do whatever you can to uproot it. This one takes work, but God will help you.

HELP THOSE WHO ARE DEALING WITH ANGER, BITTERNESS, OR UNPLEASANT EMOTIONS

When friends begin to express unpleasant emotions, be compassionate. Ask God to give you his view of your friends when they are suffering. I received the following advice from Jan Dravecky, who had to learn to deal with a host of unpleasant emotions when her husband, Dave, battled cancer, lost his career as a major league pitcher, and had surgery to amputate his pitching arm in order to remove the cancer. Now Dave and Jan have a ministry of encouragement to help those dealing with cancer, amputation, or life-threatening illnesses. They also provide support for their friends and family members.

LOVING THOSE WHO ARE SUFFERING

When I asked Jan for her advice for you, she said, "Don't judge a person who is suffering for how he bears his suffering. God uses suffering to purify us; that means it's going to bring up the dross that is under the surface in anyone's character.

"When Dave was suffering I felt compassion because I knew the heart of the man as he wanted to be. But when the pain gets to be unbearable, a guy can't be the man he wants to be. Even the most spiritual man is able to act spiritual short term when he is hurting, but long-term pain brings out the worst in any man. God knows that; sometimes that is the purpose of allowing suffering into a man's life, to purify him of all the dross. Expect it; suffering causes the uglies to come out. When you see the ugly side of him, don't be surprised! Trials are meant to bring the impurities to the surface so that God can remove them. They may bring up issues that were never dealt with from his childhood. Seeing the darkness of his soul rising to the surface may be painful for him, but that is God's business. It's God's place to deal with him. It's your place to love him."

DEALING WITH SORROW

There are times when sorrow is the only appropriate response to what is going on. While you may be inclined to quote, "Rejoice in the Lord always. I will say it again: Rejoice!" (Philippians 4:4), we must not forget that there are also admonitions in Scripture that tell us to weep and lament. Ecclesiastes 3:1, 4 says, "There is a time for everything, and a season for every activity under heaven: . . . a time to weep and a time to laugh, a time to mourn and a time to dance." Scripture also tells us to, "Rejoice with those who rejoice, and weep with those who weep" (Romans 12:15, NASB). Do not reprimand your friends for their sorrows. Instead share them.

ALLOW FRIENDS TO EXPRESS THEIR DEEPEST EMOTIONS WITHOUT REPROACH

Sometimes friends will need to vent their feelings. If they know that they can speak honestly to you without getting a negative reaction, they will find a source of comfort in you. This is one lesson I learned from experience with my husband. He shared the feelings he knew I would accept, but he often reserved feelings that were uncomfortable or difficult to bear.

At one point I asked him why, and he said, "Whenever I share what's really going on inside of me, you react. You don't just listen, you either get upset, defensive, fearful, or you try to correct how I'm feeling. If I express doubts, you immediately try to banish them. When I'm feeling uncomfortable feelings, I don't need an adjustment from you. I just need to talk things out. If you want me to share deeply with you, you're going to have to let me know that I'm not going to get a major reaction, a sermon, or a lecture."

After this explanation, and a few times when he was able to point out this kind of reaction when he was trying to share his heart, I understood. It took practice, but I learned to listen and care—and not demonstrate a major reaction. This has caused him to feel safe to open up. As a direct result, our communication deepened and he became better able to share all his feelings more freely.

DEALING WITH DEPRESSION

At some point while your friends are going through their ordeals, they may show symptoms of depression. Because the causes of depression vary, help them deal with the symptoms by helping them assess the cause. Do not simply tell your friends that Christians should not be depressed. That only adds condemnation and will cause them to with-draw. Instead, seek to understand what may be causing the depression and help your friends seek appropriate help.

The symptoms of depression include:

- sleep disturbances (either sleeping too much or not being able to sleep)
- low energy
- loss of interest in things that used to be pleasurable
- lowered sex drive
- feelings of hopelessness and worthlessness
- feeling sad and empty
- uncontrollable crying (crying every day for more than two weeks)
- loss of interest in normal activities
- noticeable shift in behavior from the way the person usually acts
- constant fatigue
- slowed or monotonous speech, hesitation to speak, or cessation of speech
- appetite changes
- physical aches and pains that have no identifiable cause
- difficulty concentrating
- intensified feelings of guilt, both legitimate and unfounded
- inability to make even simple decisions
- difficulty functioning socially
- neglect of personal needs and hygiene
- thoughts of death or suicide

While these symptoms may be common, their causes can come from various sources. The way to deal with depression will depend on the con-tributing factors causing it.

According to Stephen Arterburn of New Life Clinics, there are five general categories of depression. He writes, "Depression can be identi-fied by or classified into five basic categories. The five general categories are (1) melancholic type personality, (2) normal depression, (3) major depression, (4) manic depression, and (5) organic depression."[2]

There are some people whose personalities are such that they tend toward depression; this is the first category, melancholic-type personality. If a friend has this tendency, difficult ordeals will tend to make him or her depressed. Your friend will need your help to balance out the sadness and find hope.

"Normal depression" occurs in circumstances in which any normal person would feel depressed. If a friend is going through a tremendous loss, it will be normal to grieve that loss, which involves a time when he or she will exhibit the symptoms of depression. The key thing to look for in this case is whether your friend seems to get stuck in depression. The sadness should lessen over time as the grieving process progresses. If it makes sense for your friend to be depressed under the circumstances, encourage him or her to grieve and move through the grieving process.

"Major depression" is also referred to as clinical depression, which has a biochemical basis. This kind of depression is more than just feeling down in the dumps. Long-term stress often causes biochemical imbalances in the brain that result in clinical depression. If this condition exists, it can take medical care to get well again. Certainly emotional and spiritual conditions play a role in major or clinical depression, but there is a physical element that must also be considered. When someone is dealing with clinical depression he or she needs a combination of medical, spiritual, and psychological help.

The fourth category, "manic depression," is also called bipolar disorder because it is a physical condition that causes a person to have moods that swing between two poles: extremely high (manic) and up emotionally to extremely low (depressed) and down emotionally. This condition can be hereditary and is treatable with medication. The Christian who suffers from manic depression needs to get both spiritual and medical help to bring emotional balance. If a friend has a manic-depressive condition and is going through something extremely stressful, the underlying condition can make the highs higher and the lows lower. This is why it is important to encourage your friend to maintain contact with his or her physician as well as to get other appropriate help.

The last category, "organic depression," is depression caused by some other physical or medical cause. There are many medications that cause depression as a side effect. A person can also experience severe depression from a physical blow to the head. If your friend is depressed, his or her doctor should make sure to consider whether medication or physical events have precipitated the depression.

Remember that depression causes feelings of hopelessness and lethargy; a depressed friend will probably not be inclined to seek help. In *The Emotional Freedom Workbook,* which I coauthored with Stephen Arterburn, we offer step-by-step guidance to help your friend assess and address whatever form of depression he or she may be experiencing.

Here I feel compelled to express a word of warning to those Christians who take the stance that all depression is spiritual and should only be dealt with by spiritual means. I have seen many fine Christians deeply hurt because they were rebuffed when they dared to reach out for help. My friend Jan Dravecky was told that she could not be depressed because she was a Christian, and that to let anyone know about her symptoms of depression would be "a bad witness." Therefore she hid her symptoms until she no longer could. She ended up having severe panic attacks and a complete physical collapse before she dared to get the help she needed. If you believe that a friend should "snap out of it" because he or she should be a stronger Christian, I urge you to reconsider before you express such an opinion to your hurting friend. Read Jan Dravecky's book *A Joy I'd Never Known.* It tells her whole story and offers a wealth of insight and information that will help you truly help another without compromising your Christian commitment.

As you support friends through difficult situations, you will experience a whole spectrum of emotions. The most important thing you need to remember is that you can express those emotions—both pleasant and unpleasant—to God. Hopefully, you and your friends can also find some safe ways to express them to each other when appropriate. Having someone validate our emotions is of tremendous help.

You can help your friends by encouraging them to express their feelings to God. Read through the Psalms and the writings of the prophets, like Jeremiah (especially the book of Lamentations) and Habakkuk. Take note of how emotion-packed their writings are. God knows that you and your friends have deep feelings. You need to remember that God cares. Let him know your fears, your sadness, your grief. It is very therapeutic. If it helps, also consider writing out your feelings in prose, poetry, or song. If your emotions threaten to drown you, you can literally cry out to God, turn your groaning and sobbing into a prayer. God fully understands. The Bible tells us that the Holy Spirit knows how to interpret such prayers.

David is called a man after God's own heart. Of all the people in the Bible, we see in David the most wide-ranging spectrum of emotions. David wrote to God, "Record my lament; list my tears on your scroll—are they not in your record?" (Psalm 56:8). This was a man unafraid to express his emotions before the Lord. David knew that God was keeping record of all that he was feeling. Remind your friends that God truly knows and cares about what they are feeling. That should help.

CHAPTER THIRTEEN

Dealing with "Why?"

The May 3, 1999, cover of *Newsweek* said all that really needed to be said: WHY? The special edition heralded "Massacre in Colorado" across the top. The cover photo showed four teenage girls carrying each other along as they fled from Columbine High School. Their anguished expressions formed an appropriate backdrop for the huge letters that filled the center of the cover: WHY?

For days after the massacre, Larry King raised the same question whenever he interviewed anyone who claimed faith in God: "Why? How could a loving God allow such a monstrous attack to succeed ?" Over and over again he asked Billy Graham, Franklin Graham, Rev. Robert Schuller, Vice President Al Gore, the pastors from Littleton who conducted the funeral services for those slain there. Larry King asked them all; and they all tried to answer those most perplexing questions with a sound bite.

But the deep questions of the soul, matters of good and evil, issues of how the here and now collides with eternity cannot be answered with a sound bite. Still, "Why?" refuses to go away. Questions haunt the hurting ones until they find some satisfactory answer. When the news crews are onto the next hot story, when the disaster relief agencies have picked up and moved on, when Larry King has gone on to ask other questions, the people who are left to live in the aftermath of trials and tragedies must ask why. If you are a person who espouses faith in God, your friends may turn to you one day and ask, "Why?"

This is an important juncture because many people get stuck there, demanding answers from the Almighty or reacting against God out of a lack of understanding at a time when they need him most.

What you, your friends, and others believe about why you are going through trials will affect how each of you responds to the situation. It can have a profound impact on the level of suffering your friends go through. As you grow in your understanding of why God allows suffering, you may become better able to comfort and encourage friends in their particular situations.

I must begin with a word of warning. It is common for the friends of someone suffering to gravitate toward the assumption that the person must deserve what is happening. It is very unsettling to think that terrible things can happen to those who truly love God or those who have done nothing to deserve it. This was the mistake made by Job's friends and made by the people of Jesus' time who wanted to blame someone for the suffering they saw. Both the Old Testament and New Testament agree that there are times when bad things happen to God-fearing or good people. Both agree that those who look on one who is suffering should not assume that person is to blame. Neither should they blame the person. Whatever you do as you wrestle with the *Why?* question, don't add to the weight of a friend's suffering by blaming or condemning him or her.

Now, let's look at seven possible sources of the trials or suffering, and possible reasons why God allows suffering; these are clearly seen in Scripture. Understanding them will help you respond wisely to your friends' situations and to God as you watch friends go through trials and suffering. These things do not operate independent of each other; usually more than one is involved in any trial or season of suffering. However, you and your friends can trust that God knows how to weave them all together for good to those who love him. And in some instances, understanding the source of the trial will suggest how a friend may get through it or hold up under the pressures it brings. These seven reasons are given below in no particular order.

1. *Some trials may fit into a larger scheme of things that we are not able to see fully.*

When Joseph, the son of Jacob, was sold into slavery by his brothers, they meant it for evil. They were trying to rid themselves of him because he had visions that God would raise him up to rule over them. Then he was sent to the house of Potiphar in Egypt, where he was falsely accused of trying to rape Potiphar's wife. This led to his being unjustly imprisoned in Pharaoh's dungeon. He remained imprisoned for thirteen years. After eleven years, two of Pharaoh's servants were thrown into prison with him. Each had a strange dream, and Joseph was given the interpretation. One man would be executed, the other restored to his position. This happened precisely as Joseph predicted. The man who was restored to his position promised to tell Pharaoh that Joseph was unjustly imprisoned. But once he was out of prison, he forgot—for two years—until Pharaoh needed someone to interpret two strange dreams he had. Then the ex-prisoner recalled Joseph, who was still in the dungeon.

When Joseph was brought before Pharaoh, God gave him the interpretation of both dreams. These predicted seven years of abundance, followed by seven years of severe drought. Pharaoh recognized the Spirit of God at work in Joseph and elevated him to second in command over Egypt. He was also to oversee storage and distribution of all grain.

This brought Joseph into the position God had prophesied concerning him—the very same prophecy that prompted his brothers to despise him. Several years later, when they ran out of food, his brothers bowed before him—also as prophesied. This in turn forced Joseph's father Jacob (AKA: Israel) to move to Egypt with his entire family, which in turn fulfilled a prophecy God had given Abraham (Joseph's great- great-grand-father), which is recorded in Genesis 15:12–14: "As the sun was setting, Abram fell into a deep sleep, and a thick and dreadful darkness came over him. Then the Lord said to him, 'Know for certain that your descendants will be strangers in a country not their own, and they will be enslaved and mistreated four hundred years. But I will punish the nation they serve as slaves, and afterward they will come out with great possessions.'"

This shows us that Joseph's trials and suffering were part of a much larger scheme of things that he had no way of fully comprehending. The Psalms give us a glimpse of how God saw the years of Joseph's anguish in light of his greater plan. Psalm 105:16–19 says, "He called down famine on the land and destroyed all their supplies of food; and he sent a man before them—Joseph, sold as a slave. They bruised his feet with shackles, his neck was put in irons, till what he foretold came to pass, till the word of the Lord proved him true." Notice that God's view is that he *sent* Joseph, even though he was willing to use the plans that his brothers meant for evil.

Because Joseph had faith in God and God's promises, he did not despair in the midst of his sufferings. Instead, he was able to accept whatever came and live his life fully, even while imprisoned unjustly. He was able to work to the best of his ability whether he was working for his father, working as a slave, or working in prison. Even though much of his suffering came at the hands of those who intended evil against him, it had to pass through the hand of God. Joseph didn't know how these seemingly terrible and unfair events could lead to what God promised, but God knew. And Joseph came to understand this at some point.

We see this in Joseph's response to his brothers after his father died. They thought that he would punish them for selling him into slavery and almost killing him when he was a teen. "But Joseph said to them, 'Don't be afraid. Am I in the place of God? You intended to harm me, but God intended it for good to accomplish what is now being done, the saving of many lives. So then, don't be afraid. I will provide for you and your children.' And he reassured them and spoke kindly to them" (Genesis 50:19–21). In retrospect, Joseph could see how their evil deeds were used by God to raise him up to the position of power God planned for him.

It may be that God is allowing what your friends are going through because in the larger scheme of things, it will lead to the fulfillment of greater plans. You will probably not be able to see the whole picture as they go through the difficult trials. That is why faith in God is so important; it can give people hope while they are still in the dark about God's plans.

2. *Some suffering and trials come our way because we live in a fallen world.*

Life is often not fair, and things don't work out the way we know they should in a perfect world. King Solomon addressed this in the book of Ecclesiastes: "I have seen something else under the sun: The race is not to the swift or the battle to the strong, nor does food come to the wise or wealth to the brilliant or favor to the learned; but time and chance happen to them all" (9:11). Yes, accidents happen—even to Christians; and sometimes injustice wins out temporarily—even in the lives of those who love God.

This is important for you to realize as a friend because of how human nature tends to cause us to react when bad things happen to God's people. It would be simpler to understand suffering if God only let tragic things happen to those who deserve it. This was the error Job's friends made. They looked at how terribly their friend was suffering, and, even though they could not point to anything he had done to deserve it, they assumed he must have some secret sin that made him eligible for disaster. In the end, these friends were chastised by God for blaming Job unjustly.

This is also an error Jesus sought to correct in the thinking of his disciples.

Now there were some present at that time who told Jesus about the Galileans whose blood Pilate had mixed with their sacrifices. Jesus answered, "Do you think that these Galileans were worse sinners than all the other Galileans because they suffered this way? I tell you, no! But unless you repent, you too will all perish. Or those eighteen who died when the tower in Siloam fell on them—do you think they were more guilty than all the others living in Jerusalem? I tell you, no! But unless you repent, you too will all perish." (Luke 13:1–5)

Sometimes accidents and injustices happen to people. That is not to be taken as evidence that God loves those people less than others who happen to escape. Don't be mistaken into thinking that whatever has happened to your friends is a sign that God does not love them or is punishing them for some unknown sin. Instead, trust that even if your friends have been victims of an accident or injustice in this fallen world, God can redeem the situation. In the case of injustice, God promises that he will bring justice to all who seek it from him. So if friends seem to be suffering unfairly, don't blame them. If they are subjected to injustice, do all you can to help them seek justice; but bear in mind that sometimes justice is delayed until God makes all things right.

3. *The Bible also tells us that some of what people go through is influenced by the spiritual warfare that goes on all around us in the invisible realm.*

The Bible says that Satan is real, and that he comes to kill, steal, and destroy (see John 10:10). It tells us that our enemy, the devil, "prowls around like a roaring lion looking for someone to devour" (1 Peter 5:8). These are not pleasant experiences when translated into our lives.

All true children of God—especially those who are accomplishing things for the kingdom of God—will be subjected to the schemes of the evil one. They may undergo suffering that comes as a result of satanically inspired events. The apostle John wrote, "We know that anyone born of God does not continue to sin; the one who was born of God keeps him safe, and the evil one cannot harm him. We know that we are children of God, and that the whole world is under the control of the evil one" (1 John 5:18–19). Herein we see that the evil one cannot do us any harm unless God allows him to. However, we also see that the whole world system in which we live is under the control of the evil one. Within this context, there can be people and other spheres of influence that are directed against us by Satan.

You can help your friends by praying against any forces of evil attempting to "kill, steal, and destroy." You can join them in spiritual warfare using "the sword of the Spirit," which is the Word of God. Scripture instructs us to "take up the shield of faith, with which you can extinguish all the flaming arrows of the evil one" (Ephesians 6:16). Therefore, your continued reliance on the Lord, your prayers, and your use of God's Word to encourage your friends will all help when their suffering is partially or wholly due to a spiritual attack on their lives.

There are times when it seems that evil prevails. When Cassie Bernall was asked—at gunpoint—if she believed in God, good and evil faced off. When Cassie replied, "Yes, I do believe in God" (some report her to say "Yes, I believe in Jesus"), the gunman reportedly said, "There is no God!" before shooting her point-blank. Did evil prevail? Only if you believe that the gunman is right. Jesus said, "I tell you, my friends, do not be afraid of those who kill the body and after that can do no more. But I will show you whom you should fear: Fear him who, after the killing of the body, has power to throw you into hell. Yes, I tell you, fear him" (Luke 12:4–5).

If God does pronounce judgment and mete out eternal rewards and punishment in the afterlife, our view of this encounter broadens into the light of eternal hope and justice. Scripture assures us that death is not the end, saying, "For the perishable must clothe itself with the imperishable, and the mortal with immortality. When the perishable has been clothed with the imperishable, and the mortal with immortality, then the saying that is written will come true: 'Death has been swallowed up in victory'" (1 Corinthians 15:53–54). If we believe—as Cassie did so bravely—that God reigns eternal in the heavens, then evil did not prevail in this showdown.

4. *The Bible also teaches that trials and suffering are allowed by God to purify our faith, to purge out whatever within is not holy as God would have it.*

Scripture uses the analogy of purifying precious metals, where extremely hot fires melt the metal so that the impurities rise to the surface. Then as the metal cools, the impurities are removed from the surface. Repeating this process makes it even more pure and increases its worth. This is what Peter referred to when he wrote to the persecuted early church, saying, "In this you greatly rejoice, though now for a little while you may have had to suffer grief in all kinds of trials. These have come so that your faith—of greater worth than gold, which perishes even though refined by fire—may be proved genuine and may result in praise, glory and honor when Jesus Christ is revealed" (1 Peter 1:6–7).

When people go through suffering or prolonged uncertainty that tries their faith, what lies beneath the surface of their character becomes apparent. These may be bad attitudes, insecurities, issues from childhood that still trouble them, bitterness, inclination toward a particular sin, resentments, unresolved anger, unforgiveness, a lack of trust in God's goodness. The list goes on and on. God knows what is left within each of us that is not in keeping with the person he is making us to be; and he knows exactly what can turn up the heat to bring those things to the surface.

When the heat is on and your friends are suffering, the impurities in their lives will come to the surface. They should not try to avoid them or push them back down! No! God is the refiner; he wants to take away the dross and intended to all along. We dare not waste our pain! God allowed the heat *to bring these issues to the surface*. The best thing your friends can do is to acknowledge them, confess any sinfulness they become aware of, and ask God to take away the dross.

You may be in a position to see your friends at their worst. You may witness outbursts of anger. You may be the one to whom they confess their lapses into sin while seeking solace from the pain. You may notice the bitterness, resentment, lack of faith, or whatever God is trying to deal with in their lives. When this happens, don't be surprised and don't condemn. Instead, remind your friends that God can use this time of suffering as a time of purification as well. Pray for them in the areas where you perceive they need to ask for God's help. Be patient and compassionate. The last thing people who are suffering need is to have someone point out how poorly they are handling it.

5. *It is possible to suffer for doing good, for standing up for what is right in the face of an evil person, society, a ruler, or a system that is wrong.*

We see examples in Scripture of John the Baptist being imprisoned and beheaded for speaking against the sins of King Herod; the prophets were persecuted and killed for speaking God's Word with boldness in the face of apostate religious and political leaders; all of the apostles except one were put to death for their faith. Throughout history, Christians and God-fearing people have suffered persecution from the world.

Jesus said, "Blessed are you when people insult you, persecute you and falsely say all kinds of evil against you because of me. Rejoice and be glad, because great is your reward in heaven, for in the same way they persecuted the prophets who were before you" (Matthew 5:11–12).

DON'T BE SURPRISED!

When the Christians in the first-century church were suffering persecution, Peter wrote them saying,

> Dear friends, do not be surprised at the painful trial you are suffering, as though something strange were happening to you. But rejoice that you participate in the sufferings of Christ, so that you may be overjoyed when his glory is revealed. If you are insulted because of the name of Christ, you are blessed, for the Spirit of glory and of God rests on you. If you suffer, it should not be as a murderer or thief or any other kind of criminal, or even as a meddler. However, if you suffer as a Christian, do not be ashamed, but praise God that you bear that name." (1 Peter 4:12–16)

The approach Peter took with his dear friends is the same you should take with yours. Beware of a common error many Christians make when they see a fellow believer suffering for something that is not his or her fault. If one holds a simplistic view that bad things happen as a result of deserving bad things, or that good things always happen to good people, the inference would be that anyone who suffers does so because he or she has done something wrong to deserve it. This common mistake in theology leads to those who are suffering for doing right being mistreated by the church.

God's Word makes it clear that there will be times we suffer, not only for not doing wrong, but also sometimes for doing right. Don't assume your friend is suffering for wrongdoing. If he or she is suffering for doing right, encourage your friend as Peter did his:

. . . "Do not fear what they fear; do not be frightened." But in your hearts set apart Christ as Lord. Always be prepared to give an answer to everyone who asks you to give the reason for the hope that you have. But do this with gentleness and respect, keeping a clear conscience, so that *those who speak maliciously against your good behavior* in Christ may be ashamed of their slander. *It is better, if it is God's will, to suffer for doing good than for doing evil.* (1 Peter 3:14–17, emphasis mine)

6. *Some suffering and trials do come as the consequences of what we have done wrong.*

As surely as the natural realm operates under the natural law that "every action has an equal and opposite reaction," the spiritual realm operates by the spiritual law that says what we give out will come back to us in kind. Even though God redeems, we also see that God holds us accountable. The apostle Paul stated it bluntly, "Do not be deceived: God cannot be mocked. A man reaps what he sows" (Galatians 6:7). Jesus stated it this way, "For in the same way you judge others, you will be judged, and with the measure you use, it will be measured to you" (Matthew 7:2).

It does no good to argue with the law of gravity, rather it is wise to learn to work with it, not against it. So, too, the law of sowing and reaping. If this suffering is something your friends are reaping because of what they have sown, it does no good to pray that they will not have to reap it. Instead, pray that their hearts will be contrite as they reap what they must. Pray that they will learn from the sorrow they have brought on themselves and their families. The Bible says, "Godly sorrow brings repentance that leads to salvation and leaves no regret, but worldly sorrow brings death" (2 Corinthians 7:10). If a friend realizes that what he or she is going through is the result of going down the wrong path of life, urge repentance. You can also encourage your friend that as life does turn around, God can help him or her end up with no regrets. Such is the grace of God.

7. *The last reason for some trials and suffering is that God may be administering discipline for the purpose of correction.*

There are times God punishes us for our sins and corrects us as a father corrects a disobedient child. People tend to have strong prejudices concerning this idea. Some people gravitate to it as the explanation for all suffering. When anything bad happens, they immediately think God is punishing someone who must have done something sinful to deserve such pain. Others take offense at the thought that a loving God would dare to "punish" his children. In this matter, one's view of "discipline" or "punishment" will likely be influenced by the way that person was disciplined or punished as a child. Those who were abused may immediately associate God's discipline with something God never intended to happen to any child. However, we should not let our personal prejudices or childhood experiences warp our understanding that there are times God will discipline his children.

When God disciplines us, it hurts! But look at God's purpose in allowing painful discipline to come into our lives. I will highlight God's purposes in the passage below:

And you have forgotten that word of encouragement that addresses you as sons:

"My son, do not make light of the Lord's discipline, and do not lose heart when he rebukes you, because the Lord disciplines those he loves, and he punishes everyone he accepts as a son."

Endure hardship as discipline; God is treating you as sons. For what son is not disciplined by his father? If you are not disciplined (and everyone undergoes discipline), then you are illegitimate children and not true sons. Moreover, we have all had human fathers who disciplined us and we respected them for it. How much more should we submit to the Father of our spirits and live! Our fathers disciplined us for a little while as they thought best; but *God disciplines us for our good, that we may share in his holiness.* No discipline seems pleasant at the time, but painful. Later on, however, it produces a harvest of right-eousness and peace for those who have been trained by it.

Therefore, strengthen your feeble arms and weak knees. "Make level paths for your feet," so that the lame may not be disabled, but rather *healed*. (Hebrews 12:5–13)

God's purpose is not to punish us with pain so that we'll know how bad we are! God's purpose is holiness and healing! You should remind your friends of this. When we are being disciplined by God, the best thing to do is to look for the lessons God may be trying to teach us and then coop-erate fully. If a friend realizes that what he or she is going through is partly God's discipline, you can help your friend process the lessons in keeping with what the Bible teaches. You can also help your friend get past blam-ing him- or herself and start cooperating fully with God.

The last two reasons why we may suffer tend to overlap. We reap the consequences of our wrongdoing, and God uses those consequences to discipline us and appeal to us to repent. If you see friends going through trials for these reasons, you will need to become well versed in the lan-guage of grace to encourage them along the way. Those who are suffer-ing because of what they have done or failed to do, those who cause suffering to their loved ones, are prone to deep regrets. At some point in their journey they will be tempted to despair. At these times godly friend-ship and reassurance of God's grace will be essential.

HOPE! EVEN FOR THOSE
WHO BRING SUFFERING ON THEMSELVES

I share this story to help you offer your friends hope and reassurance in the wonderful grace of God—even when they go through hell and put others through hell by their sin or misdeeds. I had to befriend my hus-band as we suffered a terrible ordeal because he had been unfaithful. As a result of his actions, we lost our positions in ministry and our lives took a course that seemed to lead him away from fulfilling his aspirations to use his musical gift professionally.

One night, many years after going through the worst of what we went through, I was upstairs working at my computer when I heard Patrick singing downstairs. Patrick sings all the time, but this was different. He was singing to his performance tapes, which I hadn't heard him do in a long time. He graduated from Pepperdine with a music degree. When we first married, he had aspired to a career in musical theater. When we were on staff at the church, he performed regularly, as part of the worship team, doing special music, and in the large-scale musical theater productions our church produced for the community. Singing is his gift and his joy. When he was fired from his position at the church there were many years when I didn't hear him singing at all.

In more recent years Patrick has sung occasionally at our local church, but not like he used to. And his dreams of using his gift for the Lord have been all but snuffed out. We don't talk about this much, because it fills him with remorse and makes me very sad. He sees this as part of what he lost as the result of his sin. I first fell in love with him when I heard him singing, and—most of all—I love to hear him singing about the Lord. So, when I heard him downstairs singing to his old performance tapes, it touched me deeply. I sat upstairs for a while and listened, not wanting to interrupt whatever was happening with him. Then I asked if he would mind if I came down to listen.

I sat across the room as he sang a few of the old, familiar songs that brought back bittersweet memories. The sweetness came from the way things had been before his fall, and the bitter edge came from realizing all the suffering that he (and we) had been through in the interim because of what he had done, how the church handled it, and how the Lord seemed to discipline him.

I asked Patrick what prompted him to sing like this and what was going on inside of him. He grew quiet, then he said, "I was just remembering, and wondering what I might be doing with my singing if I hadn't ruined everything. I was thinking back over every turning point in my life when I made the wrong turn. I was trying to imagine what life would be like if I had made right decisions at those points. I was trying to imagine what our lives might be like if all the dark threads of my sinful choices were removed.

"As I was thinking this way, it was as if the Holy Spirit challenged me to go ahead and try to think of what life would be like if I had not made those wrong choices. Every time I tried to imagine removing a dark thread from my past, I found that God had tied it into so many good things he did in us and our lives, that all the good we now enjoy would unravel even if I just removed the worst of the 'dark threads.' So finally, I just gave up and gave thanks to the Lord. God has so redeemed all the sin and suffering I caused that I could not find one thread of it that I would remove—now—even if I could."

Somehow, God had used every wrong move, every sin, every mistake, and every bit of suffering we had endured to weave a beautiful tapestry of redemption. Our God is a redeemer. Whatever troubles your friends are facing, whatever suffering comes their way, from whatever source, God can weave it into something good. Don't ask me how because I can't figure it out even in retrospect. I only know that God does. I know this from the testimony of lives in the Bible, and I know it from what God has done in our lives. If you know this, tell your friends. If they know it, remind them when they begin to tear themselves apart and lose hope. Knowing and believing this up front will make going through the suffering and enduring the trials a far better experience.

WOULD GOD ALLOW THE BLAMELESS
TO SUFFER WITH THE GUILTY?

Another mystery human beings struggle with is why God would allow innocent people to suffer with the guilty or why God would allow innocent people to fall prey to evildoers. Why would God allow innocent children to suffer at the hands of sexual predators? Why would God allow a

Christian to be the victim of a crime at the hands of a hardhearted criminal? Why would God let a faithful spouse suffer emotional turmoil when his or her unfaithful spouse seems unruffled by ending their marriage against God's will? It's not fair! And yet these things happen every day. Somehow, we have to reconcile the harsh realities of the world we live in with the revelation of a loving God shown us in the Bible. It's not easy to address these issues—especially if it seems a friend in pain is an innocent party suffering because of what someone else did wrong—but the Bible does not shy away from such questions. Understanding how the Bible addresses this subject will help you view your friend's suffering in the light of God's steadfast love.

WHY WOULD GOD ALLOW THE BLAMELESS TO SUFFER WITH THE GUILTY?

Throughout the Bible we see God dealing with people within the context of families and nations. We see God deal with the nation of Israel and the tribes of Judah as a group. The prophet Habakkuk stood before God to address this question. He saw the righteous suffering with the wicked. He saw the innocent falling prey to the violence of those who had thrown off all godly restraint. And he demanded to know what God was going to do about it.

God didn't answer Habakkuk directly as to why he would allow such seeming injustice to go unchecked. In fact, he told him something Habakkuk found even more perplexing. God said that he was about to raise up the Babylonians to invade Judah. God himself called the Babylonians "that ruthless and impetuous people" and said they "come bent on violence." But he was about to bring his judgment on his own people in the nation of Judah who had become apostate. He was going to unleash a godless and violent enemy against them to overrun the entire country and take the people into captivity. And it wasn't just the bad people who would be taken captive. Almost everyone in the nation—good and bad—would suffer at the hands of this ruthless enemy.

Habakkuk was literally weak in the knees at such a revelation. He was dumbfounded that God could allow such a thing. But God assured him that he had it all under control. This injustice was part of the process of judging the nation's sins, disciplining his wayward people, and bringing about justice, while also separating out those who were really his from those whose hearts were not devoted to him. God would let the judgment of Babylonian captivity fall on the whole nation, but in the process he would call those who had ears to hear to turn their hearts back to him completely. Then—God assured Habakkuk—he would judge the nation of Babylon for every bit of evil it did against the nation of Judah.

What would make the difference in terms of the experience of those caught up in the wide-reaching judgment against wrongdoing? It would be their faith in God and his ability to work out a just end even when good people got caught up in the judgment of the larger group. Habakkuk is the one who first penned the saying, "but the righteous will live by his faith" (Habakkuk 2:4). He teaches us that those who have faith in God are to trust in God's providence regardless of circumstances. He declares that even if God should send suffering and loss, we are to trust that he can also bring justice in the end if we wait for him to work it out.

This sounds good in theory, but what does it look like in a person's life? Well, Daniel (as in the prophet Daniel, known for surviving a night in the lion's den) was one of the good people who was carried captive into Babylon. He is one of the few characters in all of Scripture of whom we have no record of wrongdoing. As a young man, he refused to eat the king's food because it violated Jewish dietary laws. He and his friends refused to participate in idolatry. He persisted in praying openly three times a day, even though it was forbidden by law and punishable by death in the lion's den. In Daniel we see an example of a holy life lived within the context of God's punishment for the sins of the nation.

God allowed Daniel to "suffer" captivity for the wrong that was done by the majority of the people in the nation of Judah, while also protecting and blessing him. Daniel set his heart to live righteously in Babylonian captivity, even though he had done nothing to bring the situation on himself. He was threatened and thrown to the lions, but his faith kept him safe. This is the attitude God would have your friends take also. God can protect your friends even in situations that are not of their making.

While Daniel came through unscathed, others did not. Maybe your friends weren't protected, even though they love God. Maybe your friends are suffering because some evildoer was not stopped—by God or the law. This is very hard to bear or understand. But we can gain consolation in knowing that in some cases the full delivery of what God promises will come in eternity. Hebrews 11 speaks of those heroes of the faith who:

. . . quenched the fury of the flames, and escaped the edge of the sword; whose weakness was turned to strength; and who became powerful in battle and routed foreign armies. Women received back their dead, raised to life again. Others were tortured and refused to be released, so that they might gain a better resurrection. Some faced jeers and flogging, while still others were chained and put in prison. They were stoned; they were sawed in two; they were put to death by the sword. They went about in sheepskins and goatskins, destitute, persecuted and mistreated—the world was not worthy of them. They wandered in deserts and mountains, and in caves and holes in the ground.

These were all commended for their faith, yet none of them received what had been promised. God had planned something better for us so that only together with us would they be made perfect. (vv. 34–39)

When friends are suffering for something someone else did wrong, they can be assured that God is there for them. It is very easy to turn away from God when we feel God has betrayed us by letting something terrible happen. However, God wants us to turn toward him in the midst of suffering. He will be an ally and help us deal with what has been done to us.

GOD KNOWS HOW
TO SORT OUT THE GOOD FIGS FROM THE BAD

Clear teaching on this matter is found in the book of Jeremiah, the prophet who addressed the nation of Judah before it was taken into captivity. After the king of Judah and the officials, craftsmen, and artisans were carried into exile from Jerusalem to Babylon, the Lord showed Jeremiah a vision of two baskets of figs placed in front of the temple of the Lord. Jeremiah wrote,

> One basket had very good figs, like those that ripen early; the other basket had very poor figs, so bad they could not be eaten.
>
> Then the Lord asked me, "What do you see, Jeremiah?"
>
> "Figs," I answered. "The good ones are very good, but the poor ones are so bad they cannot be eaten."
>
> Then the word of the Lord came to me: "This is what the Lord, the God of Israel, says: 'Like these good figs, *I regard as good* the exiles from Judah, *whom I sent away from this place to the land of the Babylonians.* My eyes will watch over them for their good, and I will bring them back to this land. I will build them up and not tear them down; I will plant them and not uproot them. I will give them a heart to know me, that I am the Lord. They will be my people, and I will be their God, for they will return to me with all their heart." (24:2–7, italics mine)

The prophet goes on to say whom God sees as the bad figs and what bad will happen to them. But the point that concerns you here is that you realize that God let the ones he saw as good be carried off from their homeland into captivity along with those he was punishing. To them, this was the worst imaginable course of events. They lost everything they held dear: jobs, homes, all they had worked for, loved ones, land, freedom, and human dignity. And yet God was willing to let that happen even though he said they were in his good graces. This is hard to understand unless you look at the long-term perspective.

Look at what God was going to accomplish in their lives in the process. He had only good intentions toward them. He knew that those who were still receptive to him would turn to him with whole hearts when they were in the seemingly unfair and unfortunate circumstances that had come on them as judgment for the sins of the bad figs!

Look at what God told them to do in this bad situation,

This is what the Lord Almighty, the God of Israel, says to all those I carried into exile from Jerusalem to Babylon: "Build houses and settle down; plant gardens and eat what they produce. Marry and have sons and daughters; find wives for your sons and give your daughters in marriage, so that they too may have sons and daughters. Increase in number there; do not decrease. Also, seek the peace and prosperity of the city to which I have carried you into exile. Pray to the Lord for it, because if it prospers, you too will prosper." (Jeremiah 29:4–7)

They were to settle down, cultivate faithfulness, put down roots, and live their everyday lives fully and to the best of their ability. They were not to hold back. They were to trust that God had put them in these circumstances, trust that he could prosper them—as God demonstrated in the life of Daniel—and trust that when the time was right God would bring them out and punish everyone who deserved it.

One of the most widely memorized promises of Scripture was written in a letter Jeremiah wrote to the exiles of Judah.

This is what the Lord says: "When seventy years are completed for Babylon, I will come to you and fulfill my gracious promise to bring you back to this place. For I know the plans I have for you," declares the Lord, "plans to prosper you and not to harm you, plans to give you hope and a future. Then you will call upon me and come and pray to me, and I will listen to you. You will seek me and find me when you seek me with all your heart. I will be found by you," declares the Lord, "and will bring you back from captivity. I will gather you from all the nations and places where

I have banished you," declares the Lord, "and will bring you back to the place from which I carried you into exile." (Jeremiah 29:10–14)

Consider the implications for your friends and the added comfort of knowing that this promise is particularly given to those God considered good yet were suffering judgment that fell on the group. If your friends are turning their hearts to the Lord while suffering for what someone else did or for what they brought on themselves, you can assure them, telling them this: God does still have a good plan for your life! God can bring it about and is committed to bringing it about when the time is right. You can settle down and live your life, trusting that God will not let anyone else's sin keep you from fulfilling the good plans God has for you.

HOW SHOULD YOUR FRIEND RESPOND TO GOD WHILE SUFFERING INNOCENTLY?

When suffering innocently, our first response is to turn from God. But the captives of Judah were called to not turn away from God in anger, instead to come to him, pray to him, seek him with a whole heart. God said we will seek him and find him when we search for him with our whole hearts. And he will be found. When we find *him*—not just words about him—we will have all that we need to miraculously get through anything. We will even find that one day we will be able to say that it was worth going through whatever we went through to be able to find *him* again. The restoration of that intimate relationship with God—where we have to depend on him moment by moment and can see him move on our behalf—really does make whatever we have to go through worthwhile.

EXPRESS YOUR QUESTIONS TO GOD

Your friends should not hesitate to express questions to God. If they ask you honest questions, don't reprimand them for daring to ask. This search for understanding is an important part of getting through times of suffering. Remember, Habakkuk asked his questions and received an answer—not the one he wanted, but God did respond. God is not intimidated by questions. If you don't have an answer, simply say so. You can then find someone to whom you can pose the questions or pray with your friends, asking God the questions.

TAKE YOUR SHAKEN FAITH TO GOD TOO

It is understandable that your friends' trust in God may be shaken. That may be a starting point to their discovering that God really is trustworthy. If friends ask, *How could I ever trust God if he would let me go through something so unfair?* Encourage them to rethink things. The books of Habakkuk, Jeremiah, Lamentations, and Daniel can put such questions in a larger context. If they are troubled by such questions, offer books that address these issues, such as *Disappointment with God* by Phillip Yancy or *The Problem of Pain* by C. S. Lewis. You may also want to get them in touch with a pastor who can answer some of the questions and provide enlightening spiritual knowledge.

Above all, continually ask God to help your friends understand or at least accept the things that seem too great for us human beings to grasp. Ask God to give them faith and hope that God will take care of them and that God will fulfill the good plans he has for them. Remember that it can take years for God's plans to unfold, and we may never fully understand them. So comfort and love your friends when they may not be able to see the good up ahead or understand why God is allowing them to suffer so.

RESPONDING TO OTHER PEOPLE
WHILE SUFFERING AND BEING MISJUDGED

If friends are suffering innocently, they may experience the added pain of having people react poorly. People often pull away when people are suffering because they don't want to deal with the pain. They may also feel uncomfortable with the idea that sometimes people suffer when they don't deserve to. Little is accomplished by trying to change their minds or draw them back. There will be some who naturally gravitate toward your friends and extend grace. It's best for them to take refuge in their love and try not to worry about the others.

There may even be people who will vilify your friends to make sense of what has happened. It may be easier for them to do that than to struggle with the seeming injustice of your friends' situations. Others may blame your friends unfairly. They need not accept such blame. They can ignore such people, trusting that—in time—God will clear their names. Or they can gently correct the others by stating the facts, but not arguing. These people will not be of help to your friends as they go through this. Perhaps it is best for your friends to limit contact with those who take such positions. If they are troubled by the reactions of others, do your best to offer your support and reassurance.

LOOK FOR GOD TO RESTORE WHAT HAS BEEN LOST

One of the best things to quiet a questioning mind is to see God redeem the pain your friends have been allowed to suffer. This may be especially true if your friends are suffering because of what someone else did or by being aligned with a group (family, coworkers, army, or nation) that is suffering together. When it seems that judgment has fallen from God, but we haven't done anything directly to deserve it, the best answer is to see God restore what has been lost.

This hope is present for us in the pages of the Bible. Perhaps sharing this with your friends at the appropriate time, or just praying for this to happen in your friends' lives, will help get them through. Consider the following.

Throughout the Bible, locusts were seen as a judgment from God. In any land where the people depended on their crops to sustain them, a swarm of locusts that could sweep over the land and destroy all their crops was dreaded. Locusts even came to symbolize the judgment of God. The book of Joel warned of God's coming judgment for sin, described as a plague of locusts. He called for repentance, then promised that once the people repented, God would restore all that the locusts had eaten. Joel prophesied, "I will repay you for the years the locusts have eaten—the great locust and the young locust, the other locusts and the locust swarm—my great army that I sent among you. You will have plenty to eat, until you are full, and you will praise the name of the LORD your God, who has worked wonders for you; never again will my people be shamed" (Joel 2:25–26).

Here we see that while God warned that he would bring judgment for sin, he also promised to give back all that was lost as a result. If devastation has come to your friends because of some wrongdoing or sin, God may use the loss and the negative consequences to call for repentance and renewed devotion to himself. The devastation may bring shame, but God's intention is not to leave anyone devastated or ashamed. Not only will God forgive sin, but he will also restore all that is lost as a result of sin. Even those lost to us temporarily through death will be gloriously restored to us in eternity when we experience God's promised redemption. God can use the terrible things that happen in this fallen world as a warning against sin by revealing the negative consequences sin brings. God can also restore what was lost to show his mercy, redemption, lovingkindness, and power to take away our shame.

After the prophet Habakkuk received the prophecy that God would allow judgment to fall on the entire nation because of the sin of the majority, he replied, "Though the fig tree does not bud and there are no grapes on the vines, though the olive crop fails and the fields produce no food, though there are no sheep in the pen and no cattle in the stalls, yet I will rejoice in the LORD, I will be joyful in God my Savior. The Sovereign LORD is my strength; he makes my feet like the feet of a deer, he enables me to go on the heights" (Habakkuk 3:17–19).

The deer referred to here was the mountain hind, a remarkable animal that has feet designed by God to be able to scale high, rugged cliffs. These animals can go higher on the most jagged crags because they can climb over things that would stop other animals. Not only can they go up on what looks like insurmountable terrain, but they are also able to leap from one dangerous rock formation to the next. Habakkuk here revealed that he expected God would not only bring him through the coming judgment and the suffering it would bring. He also believed that God would use the circumstances to transform him so that he would be able to handle whatever came with surefooted confidence. He knew that the Lord would be his strength.

The Lord is willing to do the same for your friends. You can't know what they will have to go through or what mountains they will have to scale. What you can know is that it will be best for them if they trust in God as they go through whatever may come. Encourage your friends to turn to God with whole hearts. Allow them to ask the hard questions without being reprimanded as if those questions reveal a lack of faith. Remind them that God is able to take care of them and their loved ones. Remind them that God will bring them through and restore their losses. In the process God will transform them so that they can experience God's strength and be able to go higher than ever before.

CHAPTER FOURTEEN

Discovering God's Purpose in Pain and the Sanctifying Power of Suffering

*I*t seems to be human nature to look for some purpose in our pain. We are not content to suffer pain as mere pain. Instead, we long to gain something from what we suffer. Vice President Al Gore told a moving story of the father of one of the young people killed at Columbine High School whispering in his ear, "Promise me that they will not have died in vain. Promise me!" God not only gives us the desire to see that our suffering is not in vain, but he also works to bring something good out of all that we suffer. God doesn't send all that causes us to suffer, but he does promise to use it to benefit those who will allow suffering to become their teacher.

In the last chapter we looked at some reasons why God allows suffering. In this chapter we will take a broader view on the purpose of pain and the benefits we can gain from the experience of suffering. Many excellent books have been written on the subject of the purpose of pain; we cannot plumb the depths of this subject here. However, this chapter can help you have a practical and biblical framework in which to view whatever your friends are going through so that you develop three things: (1) the right attitude, (2) biblical understanding, and (3) a proper response to the particular trials or suffering they are going through.

As Christians, our attitude toward trials and suffering in general should not be based on what those trials might be, but on God's command that his children can "count it all joy" when they encounter *various* trials.

Understanding the purpose of pain—even if does not come from God—and the good that can come of it can help you encourage your friends to make the best of a bad situation. It can also help you as you support your friends through whatever they are going through. Understanding the purpose behind pain will influence how you relate to your friends and how you relate to God. If you or others misunderstand the purpose, you may draw away from your friends, draw away from God, or actually interfere with his purpose in their lives.

With the right attitude and a scriptural understanding of God's greater purpose for allowing suffering, you may be better able to help your friends take the right attitude. Also, confidence that God does have some good purpose that he is working out will help all involved to persevere through whatever comes.

You may want to use this chapter simply to help yourself. Be sensitive about how and when you share this material with your friends. If they question God's purpose, that would be a good time to share whatever you find helpful. There are some times—when they are in severe pain or when they are using all their resources just to survive—when it would be inappropriate to shift the conversation to the belief that God has a greater purpose. That is true, but when friends are weeping, it's better just to weep with them. When they are ready to explore the purpose and benefits of suffering, they will let you know.

FOSTER A RIGHT ATTITUDE
TOWARD YOUR FRIENDS' SUFFERING

Your attitude toward all trials and suffering must rest in your knowledge of God as a loving, almighty, and faithful Father. If you do not believe him to be loving, you will doubt his good intentions toward your friends. If you do not believe him to be almighty, you will doubt his ability to keep his good intentions toward your friends. If you do not believe him to be faithful, you may believe he has the love and the power, but not the integrity to keep his Word.

These are basic tenets of the Christian faith that are easy enough to mouth when recounting our creed. However, when tragedy strikes, when the unthinkable happens to someone you love, when adversity comes close to home, these beliefs are tested. They are tested in the secret recesses of your heart, where you wonder, *How could a loving God allow such a thing? If God has the power to stop this, why doesn't he? God has promised us his protection; why is he letting us down?*

One of the purposes God achieves through all suffering and trials is the testing of our faith. In practice that means that suffering and tragedy actually cause us to ask these questions and persevere in our faith until we have settled them for ourselves. The Bible says, "And without faith it is impossible to please God, because anyone who comes to him must believe that he exists and that he rewards those who earnestly seek him" (Hebrews 11:6). Suffering and trials challenge our faith and give us the chance to reaffirm our belief that God exists and that he will reward those who earnestly seek him.

AN ADEQUATE FRAMEWORK FOR PAIN AND SUFFERING

Let's look at three basic scriptural beliefs that form the framework for considering God's purpose in pain and the sanctifying power of suffering. Those who hold these beliefs while they go through hell will find them proved absolutely true. I will illustrate the interrelation of these beliefs in a moment with a story, but first, let me state them plainly:

1. *God causes all things to work together for good to those who love him, who are called according to his purpose.*

While our individual purposes in life may not be clear to us at any given time, God's overall purpose for our lives is clearly spelled out. Romans 8:28 says, "And we know that in all things God works for the good of those who love him, who have been called according to his purpose."

Romans 8:29 tells what that purpose is: "For those God foreknew he also *predestined to be conformed to the likeness of his Son,* that he might be the firstborn among many brothers" (italics mine). God's purpose in the life of every believer is to have him or her be conformed to the likeness of Jesus, to become like him through whatever trials life brings. So, if your suffering friend is a Christian, then you can be assured that God's purpose is for him or her to become more like Christ through the suffering.

If your friend is not a Christian, you cannot apply this promise until he or she accepts the love of God and loves him in return. While a non-Christian cannot assume the promises made to those in God's family, God's great love extends to all. He is not willing that any should perish, but that all should come to repentance. God wants your friend to enter his family and receive the benefits of redemption—including the redemption of all his or her suffering. Whatever other purposes God is working to accomplish through these trials, you can be sure that he will use the pressures of life to offer your friend the opportunity to see his or her need for help. Your prayers and proper attitude in the midst of your friend's suffering can be used of God to bring him or her to faith, to receive the benefits of God's promise to those who love God and gain the assurance that God will work everything together for good.

2. *God does not delight in the suffering of his children, any more than any loving parent does. He only allows his children to suffer if necessary to accomplish some greater good that they may not understand.*

God is the greatest father of all; could he be calloused to the pain his children suffer? No! God cares when your friends hurt. God may be allowing them to suffer to serve a greater purpose that is not understood at the time. If you are a parent, look at how your children react when you have to take them to get their vaccination shots. They cannot understand why you allow the nurse to hold them down and hurt them, much less why you would help. You could stop the nurse! Why don't you? You can't explain it to your children at the time; but when they get older they will understand that you only allowed that pain to immunize them against the threat of a deadly disease. Were you untouched by their pain? No!

Your heart broke because of the pain they suffered—not just the physical pain but also the pain they felt at what they considered to be your betrayal when they needed you to protect them. That is the heart of God toward his children when they suffer not just the pain of the circumstance but also the deeper pain and confusion of wondering how God, who says he loves us, could allow such a thing.

3. *Nothing is allowed into the lives of God's children without his permission, even if the source of the suffering or trial is evil.*

God is not the source of all the pain and suffering that come into our lives. I don't believe God causes cancer or has any part in a rape or murder. God doesn't tempt people to do evil against others; in fact the Bible shows us that God punishes those who inflict pain on others. However, God has opted to let human beings live with free will. That free will allows people to hurt each other. There are also spiritual forces of wickedness at work in our world today. These are under the control of Satan (also called the god of this world) and seek to kill, steal, and destroy.

The Bible tells us that Satan wanted to attack Job, but he had to get permission from God before he could do so. Even then, God put limits on what Satan could do. He was not allowed to take Job's life. This cuts two ways. You may be relieved to know that God has protective limits set around your life. But it may also make you hold God partially responsible for whatever is happening. While he may not be the source of the suffering, he did allow it. To better understand this, consider not only the outcome of Job's life, but also what he learned about God in the aftermath of his suffering. The entire story is found in the book of Job.

Pain and suffering can also come from living in a fallen world where things are not as God originally intended. God decided that in order for his redemption story to be played out, he would have to take some time to re-create this fallen world. In the meantime, we live with so-called acts of God that are very destructive: tornadoes, volcanic eruptions, disease and disasters, accidents, avalanches, and the list goes on. The destruction we see that seems so senseless is part of the aftermath of the fall. This world is prone to death and disorder. God is going to remedy that, but those of us who are living in this potentially painful world must take refuge in God all our lives. Whatever the source of our suffering, nothing can touch a child of God unless God allows it through his protection.

Whatever the source, we see that God can use all the suffering this life may bring to fulfill some necessary purpose in our lives. Peter tells us, "In this you greatly rejoice, even though now for a little while, *if necessary*, you have been distressed by various trials" (1 Peter 1:6 NASB, italics mine).

Now let me tell you a story that shows the interplay of these three basic principles—(1) that God causes all things to work together for good to those who love him, who are called according to his purpose, (2) that God does not delight in the suffering of his children, and (3) that nothing is allowed into the lives of God's children without his permission and to achieve his purpose.

The Chronicles of Narnia are comprised of seven books for children written by C. S. Lewis. These fictional stories magically take several British children into the land of Narnia, which is populated with talking beasts, mythical figures, sons of Adam, and daughters of Eve (human beings). All Narnia is ruled by the great lion, Aslan (who is a figure of Christ), sent by the Emperor beyond the sea (who is a figure of God the Father). These classic children's stories are brilliantly crafted to embody biblical truth in ways that allow you to see things in story form that might have been missed when laid out directly in Scripture. Thus it was for me with the following story.

I will only describe this story from one of the Narnia books in barest detail. If you have not read the series, I heartily encourage you to do so now, and repeatedly—whether or not you have children! This story comes from *The Horse and His Boy*. The overall story is about how a talking horse and a boy prince saved Narnia from invasion. The central character is a young boy called Shasta, who is actually a prince but does not know that yet because he was kidnapped as an infant. He escapes a dreadful situation with the help of a talking horse. He is accompanied by a princess named Avaris, and her horse—who is not a talking beast. In their journeys, they meet with many dangers and trials. One of the most frightful is when they are chased by two lions, one of which scratches Avaris. They barely escape by arriving at a castle of refuge just before the drawbridge is raised for the night.

They find themselves in one trial after another, until they come to safety where Shasta discovers that he is really Prince Cor of Archenland. Without knowing it, all the trials he had been through on his journey caused him to fulfill the prophecy of his life, that he would deliver his homeland from "the deadliest danger in which ever she lay."

What strikes me about this story that illustrates our three points is the role of the lions. Near the end of the journey, Shasta finds himself accompanied by an invisible presence—a *big* invisible presence. He begs it to go away then says, "What harm have I ever done to you? Oh, I am the unluckiest person in the whole world."

The presence says that he does not count Shasta unlucky. Then he asks him to share his sorrows. So Shasta relates his sad story, especially focusing on how he and Avaris were chased by lions, and how Avaris was wounded by one of the lions. Shasta is shocked when the voice reveals that there was only one lion and says, "I was the lion."

Soon the presence becomes visible as Aslan, the Great Lion. He tells Shasta and Avaris that he was the only lion they had ever encountered. He had chased them when they needed to move faster to reach their destination. He had even wounded Avaris as recompense for the pain her actions had inflicted on another. Aslan explained to each of them why he had allowed them to be frightened, even hurt, along their journey; but he assured them that he was watching over them for their good and to bring them to their intended destination. When they asked about what would happen to others, Aslan explained that he tells no one any story but his or her own.

FOSTER A BIBLICAL UNDERSTANDING

There will be much that you and your friends do not understand about God's purpose as they go through whatever they must. It is vital that you understand and believe that God knows your friends' stories. There is much that they will not know in the midst of their trials that they may know later. There are some things they may never know because they may be parts of someone else's story. However, what we can know is that God, like the Great Lion, is with us at every point, pursuing us so he can bring about his good purpose in our lives.

There may be times when your friends are scared and confused, when they think God has surely left them to be prey to beasts. There may be times when it seems that God himself has torn your friends to pieces, and indeed when that may be true; however, you can know with absolute certainty that God loves your friends. You can take comfort in the knowledge that the God who loves us is almighty in power and faithful. If you know these things, you can be a source of stable support. If your friends also know and believe these things, they can get through anything—even when they don't understand God's purpose behind the scenes.

RESPONSE

This leads us to our final section: How can your friends best respond to the trials and suffering God is allowing in their lives, and how can you respond as one who is catching glimpses of what they're going through?

James 1:2–4 instructs us, "Consider it pure joy, my brothers, whenever you face trials of many kinds, because you know that the testing of your faith develops perseverance. Perseverance must finish its work so that you may be mature and complete, not lacking anything." Another version phrases this last verse, "And *let* endurance have its perfect result, that you may be perfect and complete, lacking nothing" (NASB).

Somehow, we are to come to the point where we can not only welcome trials into our lives, but also "consider it pure joy" whenever we face trials. The reason given is not that these trials will work out, but rather that God will use them to work something into our characters. Furthermore, we are told that we are to *let* endurance of such trials have its perfect result, that we may be mature and complete, not lacking anything. This implies that our attitudes toward each trial, and our response to it, will determine whether God's intention for the trial is completed. That sounds good, but how can we understand it to be so good that we could *actually* consider it pure joy when we encounter various trials?

That's what I'm going to try to show you here. This is a hard concept to understand and apply because we don't easily associate pain with pure joy. We don't easily associate our weakness during pain with God's strength to accomplish his good purpose for our lives. I hope this illustration will help.

When I was pregnant with my first child, someone gave me a book called *Childbirth without Fear.* It explained what would happen in labor, how my body would naturally constrict using rhythmic contractions to deliver the baby. It explained that, as labor progressed, each contraction would grow stronger, and the contractions would come closer together. It then explained that the best way to go through labor was to cooperate with the natural birth process taking place. It explained that when a woman became afraid of the pain and resisted the contractions, her muscle tension actually worked against the natural process of her body. This meant that her body would have to work harder, producing stronger and more painful contractions to accomplish the goal of delivering the baby. The author then appealed to common sense by saying that if the woman would simply relax completely, go limp, and let her body do the good work it was about with the contractions, the birth would come sooner and with less pain.

The author also suggested that the mother-to-be think of the joy she would have when she held her baby in her arms. He suggested that she think of each contraction as a wave of the sea that was meant to carry her ever closer to that joy—and the joy of having labor over with! If she struggled against each contraction, the author said that would not allow each contraction to take her as far as it could. Therefore, she was to think of becoming as cooperative as possible—not resisting the contraction or tensing up in any way.

That sounded great, and actually reduced my fear of giving birth the first time. However, while everything he said was true, when the experience of labor began in earnest, living out those simple instructions became one of the greatest challenges of my life. But I did remember what he had helped me understand about the strength of the contractions being God's way of bringing forth my baby. Therefore, when the contractions became strong, I didn't resist them. I felt as weak as I ever have before or since, but in my weakness, I relaxed and trusted that the strength of the contraction would hurt less if I just went with it. I knew the purpose of the contraction, so I chose to relax and let it do its perfect work—bringing forth my baby. While I did have to endure pain, that pain came moment by moment so that it was never more than I could bear. And all the pain had a purpose, to bring me the joy of holding my baby in my arms.

When my twenty-seven hours of intense labor ended—including having to endure abuse from a nurse I was sure came to torment me as an agent of Satan himself!—I held my beautiful daughter in my arms. Oh, the unfathomable joy of that moment! Patrick looked at me and said, "Honey, you don't ever have to go through that again. We can adopt if you want." And my response to him was, "It wasn't that bad. I could go through that again anytime if I knew I could count on this joy"—referring to my baby nursing contentedly in my arms. That's what I think James means by "count it all joy."

If you count on eventually having joy whenever God allows you to go through trials and suffering, then you are encouraged to relax in the midst of them because you know that even the pain of the spiritual contractions are part of God's plan to bring about his good intentions for your life.

In terms of sharing this information, be careful. If my husband had discounted the pain of my contractions while I was going through one, I might have hurt him—badly! It was between the contractions when I wanted to hear his reminders to me that we would soon have some joy to share when our baby was born. Find those moments in between the painful "contractions" of your friends' ordeals, and encourage them that there will be a time for joy in the future. When your friends want to talk about the possibility of God's redeeming purpose in what they are going through, having a biblical view of trials and suffering will prepare you for those conversations.

So now let's "count" some of the benefits of trials mentioned in the Bible. These are benefits we all can experience as the result of what we suffer in life. If you have these in mind, there may be times when you can help your friends discover some of these benefits by responding as best they can.

THE BENEFITS OF TRIALS AND SUFFERINGS

- We may become mature, complete, and not lacking anything. James writes, "Consider it pure joy, my brothers, whenever you face trials of many kinds, because you know that the testing of your faith develops perseverance. Perseverance must finish its work so that you may be mature and complete, not lacking anything" (James 1:2–4).
- We learn obedience through the things that we suffer. Hebrews 5:8 says Jesus "learned obedience from what he suffered." Even when we are not suffering because of disobedience, we can learn to be obedient to God in the midst of our suffering.
- Adversity can bring humility. Psalm 107:39 tells us that oppression, calamity, and sorrow can humble those God has redeemed. When we are humble, we are in the best position for God to lift us up.
- Suffering produces what God wants to develop in us. God's word says, "And we rejoice in the hope of the glory of God. Not only so, but we also rejoice in our sufferings, because we know that suffering produces perseverance; perseverance, character; and character, hope. And hope does not disappoint us, because God has poured out his love into our hearts by the Holy Spirit, whom he has given us" (Romans 5:2b–5). The character and hope God wants to produce in us are produced through suffering. So we rejoice in the

blessings of God, and we rejoice in the sufferings he allows because we know he is doing a good work in us and through us.

PRAY FOR YOUR FRIENDS TO RECEIVE THE FULL BENEFITS OF WHAT THEY'RE GOING THROUGH

If you have prayed for God to remove the trials from your friends' lives and he hasn't, there is something to bear in mind. God is not nearly as concerned with bringing us out of our trials as he is with what the trials bring out in us. Therefore, when your friends are going through trials, don't just ask God to get them out. Remember, God let your friends get in these situations or endure this suffering for a reason. Therefore, your further response to your friends' trials should be, "Lord, accomplish your purpose!" or, "Complete your inner work through this as quickly as possible so you can take it away," or, "Lord, cause my friends to relax and trust you as they go through this so that you can do your perfect work in their lives." And, "Lord, let my friends respond to you, to learn whatever you have to teach them in this trial so that you can remove it as soon as your work is complete." And, "Lord, please let my friends receive the full benefits of all that they are suffering so that their suffering is not in vain."

DON'T BE SHOCKED THAT GOD ALLOWS TRIALS

The Bible urges us not to respond to trials with surprise and shock. Trials are to be expected; Jesus promised that in this world we would have troubles. Why the shock? The apostle Peter wrote, "Dear friends, do not be surprised at the painful trial you are suffering, as though something strange were happening to you. But rejoice that you participate in the sufferings of Christ, so that you may be overjoyed when his glory is revealed" (1 Peter 4:12–13).

HELP YOUR FRIENDS LOOK FOR LESSONS
AND GROWTH FROM THEIR TRIALS

We are told to "endure hardship as discipline" (Hebrews 12:7). If your friends so choose, they can endure all that they are going through as discipline, as if there is something to be learned and gained from it. Just as an athlete experiences pain in the process of self-discipline, your friends can accept the pain as part of the process of finding the gain in their difficulties. While not every pain brings gain, we can continue to always look for possible lessons. Your friends don't have to know why a trial or suffering came into their lives to be able to learn something from the process of going through it.

Whenever it's hard to endure what your friends are going through, encourage them to switch from asking *Why?* to asking, *Lord, what can I learn from this? How can I have an attitude like Jesus in the midst of this trial?*

I know this may sound simplistic, but what seems simple is often not easy. Doing these things may be about as easy as using the breathing techniques I learned in childbirth class during real labor. But just because it's hard to do, doesn't mean it has to be complicated.

Getting through the trials and suffering that may come will test our faith, test our endurance, test our patience, and test whatever else God knows needs to be tested. But that is good! Your friends will be better able to get through their trials if they appreciate the larger purpose and choose to benefit as much as possible from them. God will be with them all the way, and friends like you can also lend support and encouragement. While the beliefs in this chapter will prove true, the challenge of holding onto these beliefs will probably not be easy. But God will bring your friends through this time better if they believe these things than if they do not.

God wants to reveal his greater purpose in a way that will comfort your friends and bring glory to himself.

The proof of our faith will be found to result in praise and glory and honor to God. Peter said our fiery trials were worth it: "though now for a little while you may have had to suffer grief in all kinds of trials. These have come so that your faith—of greater worth than gold, which perishes even though refined by fire—may be proved genuine and may result in praise, glory and honor when Jesus Christ is revealed. Though you have not seen him, you love him; and even though you do not see him now, you believe in him and are filled with an inexpressible and glorious joy, for you are receiving the goal of your faith, the salvation of your souls" (1 Peter 1:6b–9).

When we are in the trials, people are watching; when we truly believe God and take him at his word, he rewards our faith with substance. He answers our prayers and proves himself faithful in our lives. This reveals Jesus Christ to the world in a way it may not be able to understand, but cannot deny.

Even though the suffering was immeasurable, look at how God was glorified through the lives of those who died in Littleton. One girl who died was said to have desired only two things: to graduate and to have God use her life to glorify him. She didn't graduate from high school; instead she graduated to eternal life. And her testimony of faith in the Lord went out to the whole world. The funerals of Rachel Scott and Isaiah Shoels were broadcast in their entirety, poignantly celebrating the good news of eternal life to a weeping world.

No one dares to say that we accept the deadly violence, racism, hatred, and murderous rage unleashed on the students of Columbine High School (or anywhere else in our world). However, we must accept the fact that we do live in a fallen world where God has given humanity free will. When people choose to turn their hearts toward evil and their hands toward violence we must oppose it with all our moral strength and practical wisdom. But whenever there is suffering and pain, there is the opportunity for us to learn something from it and change our ways.

If the martyrdom of Cassie Bernall gives one person the courage to courageously proclaim his or her faith, her death has not been in vain. If the death of Isaiah Shoels causes one more person to oppose racism, then he has not died in vain. If the death of Dave Sanders, the teacher who laid down his life to protect his students, causes one person to look out not only for his or her own interests but also for the interests of others, he has not died in vain. I do not know what your friends may suffer, but if there is anything you or others can learn from the suffering, then the suffering has not been in vain.

CHAPTER FIFTEEN

Helping Your Friends Get Past
the Pain and Sorrow

*I*f you stay connected to your friends as they go through this difficult process, the time will come when you may be able to help them put the past behind them and get over whatever happened.

In 1997, I had the pleasure of helping Lyndi McCartney craft her insights and reflections on thirty-four years of marriage to her husband, Bill. You may know him as the founder of Promise Keepers. Bill was finishing his book *Sold Out*, in which he reflects on his entire life in view of what God has done. I was surprised to find that Bill and Lyndi weathered many crises throughout their marriage, and that Bill had been an alcoholic for many years early on. I guess we all tend to think that the people God uses greatly are somehow different from the rest of us.

In talking with Lyndi, I was reminded again of the truth Jesus taught about the storms of life in his parable of the wise and foolish builders. No one is exempt from the storms; what makes the difference in the outcome is whether our lives are built on the firm foundation of obedience to God's Word. The storms come to all, and even those who are "sold out" to God sustain damage to their lives when the storms hit. Bill and Lyndi were no different.

CAN WE EVER PUT THIS BEHIND US?

At the end of Bill and Lyndi's book, they approached the subject of putting the past behind and pressing on to the upward call of God for their lives. That's when Lyndi asked me, "Can we ever really put the past behind us? I've heard that verse quoted so many times, but I don't seem to be able to get past the past; it seems like I drag it along with me."

Lyndi brought up a significant point that you may need to address with your friends in the future. Some people never seem to get over what happened in their lives. It is possible not only to live in the past, but also to let the past ruin your future. This is never God's intention. God's purpose is to bring your friends through the valley and out of the storms, into a brighter and happier future. This isn't something that just happens though. Your friends will have to actively cooperate with God's plan to put the past behind them and press on to the good life God intends for their future.

Let me share with you what I shared with Lyndi as to how we do this. Let's stay with the imagery of a storm. As I watched newscasts showing the devastation brought on by the violent storms stirred up by El Niño, the stories followed a pattern. There were storm warnings. These were followed by the dramatic footage when the storm hit, showing the powerful winds, flooding, crashing waves, and the destruction it brought. Then there were images of blue skies overhead and a ravaged landscape of uprooted trees, destroyed houses, mud-filled cars and streets. These were used as a backdrop for reports of how many people were killed or injured in the storm. Next came the images of people working to clean up the debris—shoveling mud out of roadways, clearing away the splintered wood, hauling away the uprooted trees. These were usually accompanied by uplifting personal interest stories about the resilience of the human spirit. And several months or years later that same city will show up in the news for some other reason, but they will show the beautiful new buildings that were built after the "big storm" for which that city will always be remembered. We don't usually hear about the individual lives of all the people who were hurt and have since died or recovered from their injuries.

This is always the way it goes. When a big storm has passed, people don't just live in the muck and debris; they start cleaning up. They don't leave the injured in the streets untended; they get them to the hospital. They don't stop using the roads just because they are filled with mud. After the storm has passed, the effects of the storm have become part of the present. It's only common sense that people don't just accept their mud-filled streets as part of life and live with them. So, too, your friends are not supposed to just live with the damage of what happened as they went through hell. God intends us to remedy the damage that has happened in the past—to whatever degree we can—and press on toward a better future. That means cleaning up, rebuilding, and making sure those who were hurt are tended to and given the chance to heal. This is also how we should handle the emotional, spiritual, and practical aftermath of life's storms.

Christians sometimes misapply Paul's admonition to the Philippian church that says, "I press on to take hold of that for which Christ Jesus took hold of me. Brothers, I do not consider myself yet to have taken hold of it. But one thing I do: Forgetting what is behind and straining toward what is ahead, I press on toward the goal to win the prize for which God has called me heavenward in Christ Jesus" (Philippians 3:12b–14). They act as though we are to simply pick up after one of life's storms and go on without looking back or dealing with the damage.

This is not the intention of the passage. The word used here, *forgetting*, is not to forget as an act of the will. It means to let it slip your mind. When people go through hell, in whatever form that takes, they do not forget the events. However, they can get far enough along that whatever happened to devastate their lives does not dominate their thoughts. They can get to a point where there are times when it slips their minds.

I agree with Paul that we are to press on toward what is ahead, but the best way to move forward after a storm is to tend to the wounds of those who have been hurt, clean up the debris, and rebuild our lives according to God's design. When we do this, we will truly be able to forget the past because its effects will not be left cluttering up the streets of our present lives or impeding our way to the future God has planned for us and those we touch with our lives.

Crises will pass. When they do your friends and their families will need to assess the damage, come up with a plan to clean up the mess that has been made, and act on that plan. Your friends will have to cooperate and put some good old-fashioned work into their new way of life, relationships, and whatever else has been messed up.

CLEANING UP

The cleanup may require hard work, but what needs to be done will be apparent. Cleaning up tends to be self-explanatory because we recognize a mess when we see one. Problems usually suggest the solutions they require; it's just a matter of finding the resources and energy to tackle the job.

REBUILDING

Rebuilding after the storms is a bit more of a challenge than the initial cleanup, especially if the lives your friends knew before have been wrecked. Depending on the nature of what your friends have gone through, there may not be a way to simply repair their lives; that way of life may not be an option anymore.

At first the realization that one's life cannot go back to what it once was or was planned to be can be terribly unsettling. When we were facing this realization, one of our counselors gave that view a different spin. This may be helpful to your friends. The counselor said that perhaps one reason God had allowed life as we knew it to be blown away was that it wasn't built right in the first place. He encouraged us to stop thinking in terms of "getting back to normal" and start thinking of designing a whole new life on the foundation of our devotion to Jesus Christ. That was a freeing paradigm shift. It helped us look at our lives before the storm and assess it for its design flaws. After we had taken stock of these flaws, we prayed that God would give us a new set of plans to design a whole new life style in keeping with what he envisioned for us. That process of reassessing our life style and relationship was like sweeping the debris into a pile. Choosing to throw the old away and start fresh was like taking that debris to the dump where it belonged.

Then we began to dream again, unhampered by our past mistakes. We stopped trying to get back to where we had been and started looking forward to getting to the kind of life God meant for us to have all along. We sketched out our dreams and prayed for God to help us make them come true. We kept working to maintain our basic necessities of life, even taking jobs that were not our ideal. When we gave up aiming for the life we had lost and aimed for a good, new life, we gained momentum.

And God has made those dreams come true! We had to do the work to build that new life, but God gave us the blueprints and the resources to build it. Our new life is so much better than the one that was destroyed that there is no comparison. If it took that storm to get us to start all over again and build this new life, I thank God even for the storm!

Your friends will get past their crises. As they do, stand ready to encourage them not to limit themselves to thinking in terms of repairing the damage. Prayerfully ask God to show them if it would be better to repair or to rebuild. Ask God to help your friends see their lives in terms of becoming what God intends them to be, instead of limiting themselves to the framework of what they've known in the past. God had so much more for us than we understood at the time; he has more for your friends than they can possibly imagine on their own. Ask God to give your friends his vision.

DREAM AGAIN!

Your friends may hesitate to dream again because of all they've been through. They may focus on their limitations and how they don't have what it takes to create a new life. Before they are ready to look to the future, you can pray that God will prepare their hearts to dream again.

When the time comes when they are willing to dream, but only see their limitations, remind them that God has all they need. And God likes nothing better than to help his loved ones enter into the kind of abundant life he intends for them. Pray for the wisdom, resources, practical help, and opportunities your friends will need to build that better life. Encourage them to pray with you. That is a prayer God delights to answer.

THE PROCESS OF GETTING OVER WHAT HAPPENED

Now let's look at the process of getting over what has happened and healing those who were hurt:

HEALING THOSE WHO WERE HURT

Cleaning up and rebuilding deal with the material damage, but people are also affected by storms. Not only will your friends have to deal with the material damage to their lives in terms of practical ramifications, but they must also attend to the people who were hurt. Depending on the kind of crises your friends have endured, those affected may have physical injuries. But people were also undoubtedly hurt in other ways; it's just that the emotional, relational, psychological, and spiritual wounds can be hidden or ignored more easily than physical wounds. Just as it would be ludicrous to clean up the damage done to the physical structure of a town and leave the wounded untended, it is foolish and dangerous for your friends to put their lives back in order but neglect the hurts people experienced.

Neglecting such wounds causes the pain of the past to keep recurring in the present. It keeps people from making unimpeded progress toward the future. This may happen because your friends are afraid to face their own deep sadness, fears, disappointments, and doubts. Or they may be afraid to face how their crises have hurt the people they love most. While it may be painful to tend to the wounds, especially when your friends may experience more pain and sorrow in the process, it's worth it. It is scary; it is also necessary in order to heal.

BIND UP THE WOUNDS

Hosea 6:1–3 speaks to the necessity of healing those who are wounded as a prerequisite for pressing on to know the Lord. Hosea wrote:

> *Come, let us return to the LORD.*
> *He has torn us to pieces*
> *but he will heal us;*
> *he has injured us*
> *but he will bind up our wounds.*
> *After two days he will revive us;*
> *on the third day he will restore us,*
> *that we may live in his presence.*
> *Let us acknowledge the Lord;*
> *let us press on to acknowledge him.*

When your friends have made it through their current trials, they may feel as if God himself has torn them to pieces. Whatever your friends' perceived source of the wounds, God is committed to healing them, but your friends must present themselves to God. They must allow God to guide them to get the cleansing and tending that is necessary for the healing to take place.

Time alone does not heal all wounds. A wound left untended will get worse, not better, over the course of time. It will become infected. So too your friends' inner wounds. They should not leave them untended. Think about what happens when you see someone who has been injured. You don't stand around arguing about whether you know how that wound occurred, or who is to blame, or whether it should have happened. If you see someone in pain, you get help. That is what you can encourage your friends to do. If the crises have passed, but the pain or inner torment continues, they need to address the pain, find out what is causing it, and do something to take care of tending their wounds. This holds true whether the wounds are physical, emotional, spiritual, or relational. While time alone does not heal a wound, even a wound that has been tended and cleansed requires time to heal. Do not demand that your friends "snap out of it." Instead give them the support, help, attention, care, and time they will need to heal.

SPIRITUAL SPLINTERS

There is another kind of injury that can happen during a crisis—especially a prolonged crisis—that I call spiritual splinters. These are the small things that wounded someone initially but were not dealt with right away. These may be things that seemed too small to deal with at the time because of the pressing nature of the situation, or things your friends did when they were under duress that hurt others. These are the kinds of things that everyone seems to forget about, but they are still there. That's why I call them splinters.

I hate getting splinters! When I was a kid, I had a really bad splinter that my dad removed with a needle; it was a painful "operation." After that, I always hid my splinters. They weren't a big deal and I learned that if I kept my splinter hidden for a few days, I would forget about it. During the initial phase of having the splinter, I would favor that hand, avoid using it, and definitely hide it from my dad. Then it disappeared, and if I ever noticed it again, it didn't seem to hurt. So my policy on splinters became: Hide it and if it ever comes up again, deal with it then.

My husband is a "Get the needle, tweezers, and peroxide!" kind of guy when it comes to splinters. So when my daughter, Casey, showed me a nasty splinter in her hand when she was about eight, we conspired together not to let her dad see it. I assured her that these things have a way of "working themselves out." I poured some peroxide on it, covered it with a Band-Aid strip, and forgot about it. The Band-Aid eventually fell off, the pain was gone, Patrick was none the wiser, and the tweezers never came out of the medicine cabinet. Mission accomplished! Or so I thought.

Several weeks—maybe even months—later, Casey showed me a strange white circle that appeared on the palm of her hand. It was entirely numb. We kept an eye on it over the course of the next few days as it turned from white, to having a pink ring near the center, to having a dark dot in the center.

Neither she nor I associated it with the long-forgotten splinter, but we were curious at to the cause of this strange thing. Then it dawned on me that the unidentified black dot was appearing in precisely the same location where the splinter had gone in.

A few days later the mysterious black dot raised slightly above the numbed skin and Casey agreed to let me touch it. She felt nothing. So she agreed to let me go after the black dot with a needle. I put the needle into the raised black "dot" and lifted. A splinter almost half an inch long came out without so much as a squeal from Casey, who had her eyes closed. After I removed the splinter, her hand healed completely and the numbness went away.

I saw in this experience a similarity to something that happened in the aftermath of our crisis. When Patrick and I were in the process of getting counseling for the wounds we had suffered, I discovered areas of my life where I was completely numb. There were episodes from my past that should have been painful—particularly things from my childhood—over which I felt nothing. These were things that had happened to me when I was young that I had never revisited. When I had been hurt, I'd had no remedy, so I just hid the pain. After a while I didn't hurt when I thought about those incidents. But I was also numb emotionally and cut off from that part of my life. The counselors helped me revisit the events that had wounded me but had never been dealt with. This didn't hurt, but it did bring a deep healing that has caused me to regain feeling where I was formerly numb emotionally.

With regard to coming out of crises, there will be spiritual splinters. These are the things your friends may know have wounded them, or things they know they did that wounded others, that no one wants to bring up because it might hurt someone's feelings. There are some things that can be allowed to slide because everyone understands that people can lash out when they are under stress. But if there are areas of life that have become off limits, or completely numb, it may warrant discussion with a friend or counselor.

Sometimes ignoring significant hurts can cause us to become numb to the people we love. The numbness may have provided protection during the more pressing issues of the crisis, but the numbness can dull our experience not only of the pain but also of the ability to feel love. Sometimes it's better to deal with the temporary pain of bringing up the sensitive issues and getting rid of them than to add them to the splinter collection and risk losing the ability to feel those things that make life wonderful.

Encourage your friends to remove all the past hurts, to forgive, to make amends when necessary, to listen to how they may have hurt others, and to give every wound and splinter the attention each deserves. Yes, it hurts initially. But the healing doesn't take nearly as long as they may fear. The wonderful thing about tending to the wounds and splinters in our lives is that it helps people and relationships heal.

SCARS

Wounds and splinters require action to heal properly, but once these have been dealt with, there comes a time when your friends should stop going back to the point of injury. The process of fully grasping what has happened, how it happened, why it happened, and what it means is an important phase that can take months or years. However, there will come a time when all that has been considered, new understandings have been reached, and there is nothing more that can be done about the past. It is history. Once the wounds and splinters have been tended and healed, we are left with what I call spiritual scars.

A scar is a reminder of a wound that once occurred but has healed. If you touch it, the tissue is neither numb nor painful. It's just a visible reminder that you were once hurt in that place. You probably know exactly how you got every scar you have on your body. I can even tell you which stretch marks were created by which pregnancy! These physical scars bear silent testimony to what happened, but there is nothing left to be done other than to recall what happened. Some of the wounds inflicted during your friends' journeys through the valleys and the storms they endured will leave scars. That's OK; scars can be a reminder of survival as well as suffering.

This relates back to Lyndi McCartney's questions, "Can we ever really leave the past in the past? Can we press on toward the future without dragging the past along with us?" I answer a hearty, "Yes!" This is not to say that your friends or anyone who went through the storm with them will ever forget what happened. This is not to say that your friends' lives will ever return to "normal"—perhaps they cannot. But your friends can get to a place where they will be able to think about what they have been through and how it changed their lives. They will be able to talk about it without crying, or growing fearful, or flying into a rage, or being consumed with jealousy, or whatever emotions overcame them as they were going through the valley. Your friends can experience restoration and redemption in some way. They can become content.

Your friends can get to a place where they are at peace again, able to accept what God has allowed, able to live productive lives, able to fulfill what God created them to accomplish. God can restore to them the joy of his salvation; give them beauty instead of ashes, the oil of gladness instead of mourning, and a garment of praise instead of a spirit of heaviness. Your friends can get to the place where they can talk about their experiences in the past tense, and with a sense of acceptance and greater understanding about what God accomplished—even if they never fully understand why it happened.

I know this sounds hard to believe. During the times our family was going through hell, there were many years when I could not believe this would be possible. I was so consumed by the pain of the crisis, the battles we had to fight, the enormous toll it took on every facet of our lives. But I had a few good friends who stayed by me, confident that I would get over what happened and see God restore our losses. You can be that kind of friend too. You can accept your friends while they cannot see what good could possibly come of what they are going through but remain confident that God can bring something good out of any situation. When the time comes to rebuild a new life, you can encourage them to do so and celebrate with them when they have been able to adjust to their new lives.

I can speak with confidence because we have made it to the other side of the valley. Looking back I can see how God used our friends who always reassured us that we would get through the valley. The problems that once looked like insurmountable peaks have now faded into the background of our history. Sure, we can still look back and see what happened. But, when seen in the light of what God has done since, the problems God empowered us to overcome are on the far horizon. While we were going through the valley, especially when the storms were raging, we couldn't see this far ahead. Our friends were the ones who encouraged us to keep pressing on.

I don't know what problems or suffering your friends are going through that caused you to pick up this book. I do know that God is faithful, regardless of what your friends are facing. I do not know what is at stake in your friends' lives or the wounds they have suffered. I do know that every wound hurts, that every battle that threatens our lives will be hard-fought, and that every threat to your friends, their families and their God-inspired dreams is worth fighting fully. I also know that God does not intend for his children to be defeated. I encourage you to stand firm in your faith, for your friends' sake. Enter the spiritual battle on their behalf. Encourage them to stand firm and to rely on the power of Almighty God. While your friends will not come out of the battle unscathed, God can even use the scars for his glory. God knows, there are battles to be fought. And battles to be won!

Once I shared with a group of women about the battles my husband and I have had to fight to preserve our marriage. One wrote me a note that said, "Many marriages have suffered much less and fallen apart. . . . God is willing to invest in marriages in pain, but it seems *people* aren't. We need you. I don't want to hear from the General in the office. I want to hear from the soldier who is seasoned, who has survived, who is standing next to me with scars from battles won."

I gained credibility with this woman because I have seen battles in this life and have survived—by the grace of God. What she did not note was that my husband and I did not battle alone. We had a small band of friends who made our battle their battle. They were there for us with spiritual, emotional, and practical support. When we were wounded, God used them to bandage our broken hearts. When we were broke, God used them to help us out financially—without ever causing us additional shame. When we were going through the uneventful times when the crisis was over but the recovery had just begun, they brightened up our lives. When we made progress, they came to celebrate with us. And they always held on to heaven and petitioned God on our behalf.

Yes, we will all face battles in life. And we will all bear the scars. But when our Christian friends stand by us, love us, and fight with us, we will also share the victory! You can be that kind of friend. You can see your friends all the way through this—with some level of involvement. You too can see them come through stronger, happier, more confident in God, vibrant, and full of encouragement for others!

My most notable season of "going through hell" began shortly after my thirtieth birthday. The next decade was an amazing journey of going through the worst in life to get to the best. I don't know exactly when you could say I came out of the valley. But by the time I celebrated my fortieth birthday, we had definitely come through on the other side. So my husband brought together many of the friends who helped us along the way. What a celebration we had! There was a sense of camaraderie among us, like that shared by veterans who have won the war together. We shared in remembrance of all we had been through, the times when we saw no possible good that could have come out of what we were going through, and our amazement as God did great and mighty things on our behalf. Our celebration rang with joy, laughter, and triumphant praise of God.

One day, the spiritual battles you are fighting on your friends' behalf will be done. And they will probably bear some scars from the battles. You may too. But if you continue to hold on to heaven, and your friends do as well, God will bring triumph as you follow his commands. There may come a time when you and your friends can reminisce about all you saw them through. You may even show each other your scars, but that will not be an exercise in shared pity; rather it will be a tribute to what God has brought you through. I pray you and your friends join the ranks of those with scars from battles won. When you do, I pray that you become a source of strong encouragement to others, as others have been to me, and I pray I have been to you.

EPILOGUE

You Can Make a Difference!
The Far-Reaching Power of Friendship

Thirteen-year-old Bill Wilson walked down the block with his mother. They'd had a hard year. They sat down together near a drainage ditch. Then she said to him, "I can't do this anymore. You wait here." She left and didn't come back. Bill didn't know what to do. He had nowhere to go. So he just sat there—for three days. People passed by, but no one reached out to him. On the third day, a Christian man walked by and recognized Bill as a neighbor. He could have easily passed by, too, but he didn't. Bill says, "He stopped, picked me up, got me some food, and paid my way to a Christian camp." That's where Bill Wilson accepted Jesus Christ as his Savior and Lord. That was many years ago; but that one act of friendship continues to have positive impact on the lives of thousands.

Today, Pastor Bill Wilson is Senior Pastor at Metro Ministries International, in one of the most dangerous parts of America. In the course of his ministry he has witnessed twenty-one people killed in front of him, but he continues to pour out his heart to rescue the up and coming generation. Their strategy is to reach kids in this dangerous neighborhood and befriend them while there is still a chance for them. Bill says, "It's easier to build boys and girls than to repair men and women." Metro

Ministries' aim is to take one generation and say, "This is where it changes!" The church's mega-Saturday/Sunday-school programs reach thousands of kids each week. Bill, his dedicated staff, and committed volunteers drive church buses around to reach families on the mean streets, the inner city, picking up kids to come to their meetings. During the week they follow-up with a visit to the homes of kids who attended. In this way they also reach out to the parents, seeking to build relationships with them. They also developed Sidewalk Sunday School, an innovative program using specially modified trucks which turn vacant lots into churches for kids. Are they making a difference? You better believe they are!

One young man who had previously assumed he would be dead in less than two years in this neighborhood, gained hope for the future through the ministry of Metro. When asked how his life changed, he said, "Since I was shown love and people cared for me, I'm able to do that for others." Look at the pattern here: a man befriended young Bill Wilson when he was troubled. Pastor Wilson's ministry reached this young man when he was troubled. People in the church loved him and showed that they cared about him. Now, he can reach out with love and care for others who don't yet have such hope. It's working!

Pastor Wilson traces his far-reaching, life-saving, and transforming ministry back to that one moment when a Christian man stopped and cared. That motivates him to do the same for others. He says, "When I pick up the kids on my bus, I'm picking up me." He is living proof that one person's kindness and friendship, coming when needed most, can make a world of difference. It can give hope and help to the one befriended; but it can also go on to do more. An act of Christian friendship is like a pebble dropped into a pond of life with ripples that reach into eternity. The effect of such love and caring emanate from that one life in ever enlarging circles of friendship that can change the world.

We live in a world where rampant evil and violence cause us to ask what we can do to make a difference. Perhaps one thing each of us can do is to commit ourselves to offer kindness and friendship to those who are deeply troubled or rejected. Who knows if such acts of Christian friendship could turn someone around before they resort to violence? We don't know how much evil could be prevented with acts of kindness, nor will we know until eternity the extent of the good such kindness can do. However, Edmund Burke has said, "All that is necessary for the triumph of evil is that good men do nothing." Perhaps each one of us can do something good by being a friend to those within our reach who are going through hell.

King Solomon wrote, "Two are better than one, because they have a good return for their work: If one falls down, his friend can help him up. But pity the man who falls and has no one to help him up!" (Ecclesiastes 4:9–10).

Holding on to Heaven
While Your Friend Goes Through Hell

*W*hile this book is meant to help you help your friends directly, there was no way I could possibly deal specifically with all the possible situations your friends may be facing. One of the ways you can help your friends is to locate other resources that can help with the specific situation.

The following information is to get you started and give you general guidelines for finding help. Start with the assumption that there must be others who have gone through something similar and want to pass along what they have learned or experienced. Your goal should be to locate some of these people or organizations, check to make sure they do not violate your Christian principles, then connect your friend with the help they may have to offer.

Here are some ideas of where you can start in your search for additional resources:

- Call your church; ask your pastoral staff if they know of any resources to help.
- Call your local Christian radio station. Most Christian radio stations interview experts who deal with a variety of problems. They may be able to refer you to people in your local community who can help.

- Do research on the Internet. You can start with a search of Christian Web sites, using a search engine to identify the issues or problems your friend is dealing with. You can also use search engines to search the entire World Wide Web for resources. Make sure you do not take what you find on the Internet as gospel. There is a lot of unsubstantiated and misguided information available online. Follow up with more research and a phone call to verify that any recommended organization or book agrees with a Christian perspective.
- Visit your local library. Ask the research librarian to help you find books and resources dealing with the issues your friend is facing.
- Contact any of the following agencies.

Focus on the Family: This is a great resource in the Christian community for many different needs. They have trained counselors on hand who can speak to you. They can also refer you to someone in your area that can help you. You can reach them at (800) A-FAMILY.

New Life Clinics: When my husband and I were in crisis, this is where we turned for help. They offer expert psychological and psychiatric help within a Christian framework. They can help in times of crisis or for ongoing troubles. They can help you determine your friend's specific counseling needs and refer you to someone in your area that can help. Contact them at (800) NEW-LIFE.

Dave Dravecky's Outreach of Hope: This is a ministry dedicated to offering hope and encouragement to those who suffer from cancer or amputation. Their mission is accomplished through prayer support, personal contact, correspondence, resource referral, and the gift of encouraging literature. Inquiries may be directed to:

Dave Dravecky's Outreach of Hope
13840 Gleneagle Drive
Colorado Springs, CO 80921
e-mail: info@outreachofhope.org

The following resources are listed by category and will help you address specific areas of need. Although this list is not exhaustive, it will equip you with enough information to find help for your friend.

VICTIMS OF CRIME

"Neighbors Who Care," a ministry of Prison Fellowship
National Victim Center
2111 Wilson Boulevard, Suite 300
Arlington, VA 22201
(703) 276-2880

National Organization for Victim Assistance (NOVA)
1757 Park Road, NW
Washington, D.C. 20010
(202) 232-6682

National Victims Resource Center
1600 Research Blvd., Dept. F
Rockville, MD 20850
(800) 627-6872

Association of Traumatic Stress Specialists
7338 Broad River Road
Irmo, SC 29063
(803) 781-0017

Mothers Against Drunk Drivers (MADD)
669 Airport Freeway, Suite 310
Hurst, TX 76053
(817) 268-6233

Parents of Murdered Children
100 E. Eighth Street, B-41
Cincinnati, OH 45202
(513) 721-5683

Office for Victims of Crime
U.S. Department of Justice
810 Seventh Street, NW
Washington, D.C. 20531
(202) 307-5983

National Crime Victims' Research and Treatment Center
Medical University of South Carolina
171 Ashley Avenue
Charleston, SC 29425
(803) 792-2945

MARRIAGE RECONCILIATION

ICR (International Center for Reconciliation)
P. O. Box 1543
Modesto, CA 95354
(209) 578-HELP (4357)

Inner-City Ministry of Pastor Bill Wilson:
Metro Ministries International
P. O. Box 370695
Brooklyn, NY 11237
Web Site: www.metroministries.com
Phone: (718) 453-3352

SUICIDE

If you are concerned that someone you know may be thinking of suicide, or if someone tells you he or she is going to commit suicide, get help immediately. Call 911, your local crisis center, or the police, or take the person to the emergency room of your local hospital. Do not leave the person alone.

If the person has attempted suicide and needs medical attention, call 911 or your local emergency number. The following are suggestions for helping someone who is suicidal: Note that these are not a substitute for getting immediate help if the person is thinking of committing suicide now.

- Ask the person, "Are you thinking of suicide?"
- Ask the person how he or she intends to commit suicide. If there is a specific plan, you should take the intent seriously.
- Listen actively to what the person is saying to you.
- Reassure the person that there is help for his or her problems and reassure the person that he or she is not "bad" or "stupid" because of thoughts of suicide.
- Help the person break down problems into more manageable pieces. It is easier to deal with one problem at a time.
- Emphasize that there are ways other than suicide to solve these problems.
- Offer to investigate counseling services.
- Suggest that the person see a doctor for a complete physical.
- Try to get the person to see a trained counselor.

SOME BOOKS YOU MAY FIND HELPFUL

Helping a Neighbor in Crisis by Tyndale House Publishers is compiled by Neighbors Who Care to provide practical assistance to pastors, counselors, and others to help family, friends, and neighbors in crisis. Topics include: A Loved One Is Murdered, Crisis in the Community, Living with Physical Problems, Relationship in Danger, Victims of Sexual Crimes, A Loved One Dies, Job and Finances Are Lost, Neighbors Are Impacted by Crime, People Are Victimized, and They're Hurting Themselves.

The ten topics listed above are broken down into thirty-two crises including those dealing with burglary, child abuse, divorce, life-threatening illness, and community tragedy (like the Oklahoma City bombing). This book is available from Prison Fellowship and Neighbors Who Care or your local Christian bookseller.

Death of a Child

Gone but Not Lost: Grieving the Death of a Child by David W. Wiersbe
Surviving the Death of a Child by Frances Wohlenhaus Munday

Depression

The Emotional Freedom Workbook by Stephen Arterburn and Connie Neal
Freedom from Depression: Finding Healing and Comfort as a Child of God by Neil T. Anderson
Hand-Me-Down Genes and Second-Hand Emotions by Stephen Arterburn
How to Win Over Depression by Tim LaHaye
Spiritual Depression by D. Martin Lloyd-Jones

Divorce

Breaking and Mending: Divorce and God's Grace by Karen F. Williams
Complete Divorce Recovery Handbook by John Splinter
Helping Children of Divorce by Dr. Archibald Hart
A Passage Through Divorce: An Interactive Journal for Healing by Barbara Baumgardner

Domestic Violence

Dangerous Marriage: Breaking the Cycle of Domestic Violence by S. R. McDill and Linda McDill

Stress

Adrenaline and Stress by Dr. Archibald Hart
Balancing Your Emotions: For Women Who Want Consistency Under Stress by Gayle Roper

Stress and the Woman's Body by W. David Harger, M.D., and Linda Carruth Hager

Women and Stress by Jean Lush

Suicide

Suicide: A Christian Response: Five Crucial Considerations for Choosing Life by Gary Stewart

Notes

Holding on to Heaven
While Your Friend Goes Through Hell

CHAPTER TWO

1. Adapted from *Twelve Steps and Twelve Traditions* (New York: Alcoholics Anonymous World Services, 1953), 5.

CHAPTER SIX

1. Henri Nouwen, *Bread for the Journey*, as quoted in Lucy Shaw and Madeleine L'Engle, *Friends for the Journey* (Ann Arbor, Mich.: Servant Publications, 1997), 133.

CHAPTER SEVEN

1. C. S. Lewis, as quoted in Sheldon Vanauken, *A Severe Mercy* (New York: HarperCollins, 1977), 134.

CHAPTER TEN

1. Morton Bard and Dawn Sangrey, *The Crime Victim's Book*, referenced from *Helping a Neighbor in Crisis* (Wheaton, Ill.: Tyndale House, 1997), 10.
2. Sheldon Vanauken, *A Severe Mercy* (New York: HarperCollins, 1977), 185.

CHAPTER TWELVE

1. Dave Dravecky, *The Encourager,* Vol. 5, No. 1, Winter 1999, Dave Dravecky's Outreach of Hope, Colorado Springs, Colo.
2. Stephen Arterburn, *Hand Me Down Genes and Second-Hand Emotions* (Nashville, Tenn.: Oliver-Nelson Books, a division of Thomas Nelson, 1992), 45.

ACKNOWLEDGMENTS

Holding on to Heaven
While Your Friend Goes Through Hell

There are many people I need to acknowledge and thank for their help in bringing this book together. Thanks are due my husband, Patrick, who continually supports me in my work; to Susan Yates, who labored with me in many ways to insure that this book was the best it could be, and especially to my dear friends whose love and help sustained our family when we went through our darkest times: Rick and Kim Roberts, Rayna and Larry Bertolucci, Tracy and Cheryl Wilder, David and Debbie Darrah, Don and Diane Biggie, Gene and Jan Ebel, the youth of Heir Force 1988, and those from Little Country Church who came in and declared themselves our friends when it seemed the whole world was going out. Their active Christian love and friendship served as both model and motivation in this book. If I inspire anyone to befriend another as they befriended us, then this book has served its purpose.

Thanks to those who shared their lives and stories: Warren Shank, Dr. Mark Knoble, Dr. David George, Jayne George, Sandy Van Horn, Michelle Van Horn, Dave and Jan Dravecky, Denise Jones, Susan Yates, Michelle Williams, Dana Coats, Bill and Lyndi McCartney, Pastor Bill Wilson, the Olive Garden Girls: Lori Davidson, Lisa Lazaller, Rhonda Dotta, and Judy Thompson. Thanks also to the staff of Big Valley Grace Community Church in Modesto, California for their Women in Leadership Development conference which proved helpful.

Thanks to my agents Sealy and Susan Yates who moved this project along, the team at Word Publishing: Lee Gessner, Ami McConnell, Pamela McClure, Debbie Wickwire, Janet Reed for her fine editing, and Renee Chavez for her careful proofreading.

How to Survive when "For Better or For Worse" is Worse Than You Ever Imagined.

CONNIE NEAL

Holding On To HEAVEN While Your Husband Goes Through HELL

ALSO AVAILABLE FROM CONNIE NEAL

When a married man goes through hell, his wife is the first to feel it. Connie Neal shows women how to stand with their husbands through the storm and be a conduit for God's love and healing.

74861